Guru Gobind Singh

Hindu Turaq kou Raafazi Imaamsafi,
Maanas ki jaat sabhe eko pehchaanbo.
Karta karim soi rajakk rahim oyi,
Doosro naa bhed bhull bhramm maanbo.
Ekk hi ki sev sabh hi ko gurdev ekk,
Ekk hi saroop sabai ekkai jot jaanbo.

Some call themselves Hindu, some Turk (Muslim), some Hafzi and others Imamsafi. But the entire humankind should be recognized as one. The same One [Lord] is the Creator, compassionate Provider of bread, Munificient. He has no co-eternal, no dualism : we must never accept any duality. To serve the only One is our duty. He alone is the Guru of all. All mankind be taken as one manifestation of His light.

- Akal Ustat

BY THE SAME AUTHOR

The Encyclopedia of Sikhism (ed.) in 4 volumes

The Heritage of the Sikhs

Berkeley Lectures on Sikhism

Guru Nanak and Origins of the Sikh Faith
(also translated into Hindi and Urdu)

Guru Tegh Bahadur

Guru Gobind Singh
(Translated into many Indian Languages)

Bhai Vir Singh
(translated into Punjabi, Hindi, Sindhi and French)

Bhai Vir Singh: Poet of the Sikhs
(in collaboration with Professor G.S. Talib)

Maharaja Ranjit Singh

Aspects of Punjabi Literature

Higher Education in America

An Introduction to Indian Religions
(in collaboration with Dr L.M.Joshi)

Perspectives on Guru Nanak (ed.)

Panjab Past and Present: Essays in Honour of Dr. Ganda Singh (ed.)

Approaches to the Study of Religion (ed.)

Mahindi (short stories translated into English from Punjabi)

Sada Virsa (Punjabi)

Guru Gobind Singh

HARBANS SINGH

Bhai Vir Singh Sahitya Sadan
Gole Market, New Delhi-110001

Guru Gobind Singh
by Harbans Singh

© Estate of late Prof. Harbans Singh

First Edition   : 1966 (Guru Gobind Singh Foundation, Chandigarh)
Second Edition : 1979 (Sterling Publishers Pvt. Ltd., New Delhi)
Third Revised Edition : 2016

ISBN : 978-93-84777-83-8

Publisher: Bhai Vir Singh Sahitya Sadan
Bhai Vir Singh Marg, New Delhi-110001
Email : info@bvsss.org

Printer: Print Media
1331, Chowk Sangatrashan,
Paharganj, New Delhi-110055

Price: Please read and circulate

सत्यमेव जयते

Manmohan Singh
Member of Parliament
Rajya Sabha

MESSAGE

We are fortunate that we had the privilege of celebrating centenaries of some of the most important events of the Sikh history in our own lifetime. In 1966 we celebrated the Tercentenary of birth of Guru Gobind Singh; in 1969, Quincentenary of birth of Guru Nanak Dev and in 1999 Tercentenary of the creation of the Khalsa. I had the unique privilege of joining the celebrations at Anandpur Sahib and feeling the vibrations of the place where the Guru spent his creative years. These celebrations have not only inspired the Sikh community at home and abroad but also created awareness about our rich cultural heritage. We organized seminars at national and international level and published books under 'Panjab Heritage Series'.

To mark 350th birth anniversary of the Guru, Bhai Vir Singh Sahitya Sadan has decided to organize an International Seminar on **Guru Gobind Singh: Life & Legacy** in collaboration with the India International Centre. On this occasion, we are reprinting Biography of Guru Gobind Singh by Prof. Harbans Singh, first published by Guru Gobind Singh Foundation, Chandigarh and later by Sterling Publishers, New Delhi. We would like to thank author's daughter Dr. Nikky Guninder Kaur for her permission and for the scholarly Introduction. We would also like to place on record our gratitude to S.Harcharan Singh Nag, Vice-President of the Sadan, for sponsoring these publications for free distribution during the celebrations.

New Delhi
November 25, 2016

(Manmohan Singh)
President, Bhai Vir Singh Sahitya Sadan,

3, Motilal Nehru Place, New Delhi-110 011
Tel. : 2301-5470, 2301-8668 Fax : 2379-5152
E-mail : manmohan@gov.in

Nisan of Guru Gobind Singh from his Prayer Book
Courtesy: Bhai Jujhar Singh Bagrian

Preface

This book was first published by the Guru Gobind Singh Foundation. It was meant primarily to mark the 300th birth anniversary of the Tenth Master which fell in 1966. Besides English, the book appeared, in translation, in fifteen Indian languages–Assamese (Professor Narayan Dass), Bengali (Professor Upendra Kumar Das), Gujarati (Professor A.B. Yajnik), Hindi (Sri Devendra Satyarthi), Kannada (Dr. D.R. Bendre), Kashmiri (Sri Bansi Nirdosh), Maithili (Professor Ramanath Jha), Malayalam (Sri N. Balakrishnan Nair), Marathi (Sri Madhav Manohar), Oriya (Dr. M. Mansinha), Punjabi (Dr. Attar Singh), Sanskrit (Dr. Shrutikant Sharma, with a separate poeticized version by Dr. Satyavrat), Sindhi (Sri H.I. Sadarangani), Tamil (Professor R. Ramanujachari), and Telegu (Dr. B. Rama Raju). I render my obligations to the Guru Gobind Singh Foundation for sponsoring this book in that historic year.

For this second edition, I have made some minor revisions and additions. These became necessary, especially, in view of the new material in the form of *Bhatt Vahi* entries brought to light by Giani Garja Singh. The dates of various events now given are traceable to this source. I wish to record my thanks to Sardar Niranjan Singh who made the typescript and to Sardar Sardar Singh Bhatia and Major Gurmukh Singh, both of the Sikh Encyclopaedia Department, who helped with the preparation of the press copy. Sri Devinder Kumar Verma volunteered to compile the index. I deeply appreciate his help.

13 April, 1979   (Harbans Singh)
A-1, Punjabi University, Patiala

Prayer Book of Guru Gobind Singh with the Bagrian family.
Courtesy: Bhai Jujhar Singh Bagrian.

INTRODUCTION

Whether he was at Anandpur riding his handsome blue charger, his regal plume setting off his wiry and commanding figure, with a knightly body of devoted and daring Sikhs following him, or in the jungle of Machhiwara, barefoot and forlorn, his heart was constantly in harmony with the Divine, neither losing its qualities of love and compassion in one situation, nor giving way to despair in the other.... It is difficult to imagine a genius more comprehensive and versatile.

As this brief prelude illustrates, the impossible has been made possible: we encounter here the phenomenal personality, life and legacy of Guru Gobind Singh. It was for the 300th birth centennial in 1966 that Professor Harbans Singh undertook the writing of the Guru's biography, which provides readers with kaleidoscopic facets of Guru Gobind Singh's boundless humanity and divinity. For the author, the momentous celebration entailed an enactment of his revered Guru's moral vision: the community's "collective effervescence" was to be a recollection of the glorious Guru so that the Guru would be an essential part of their everyday sacred, social, political, economic, and cultural reality. In order to reach a wide audience Professor Harbans Singh wrote an accessible book in whose pages we intimately get to see the Guru with his resplendent plume astride his royal-blue stallion, hear his valiant melodies, feel his intense spirituality, absorb his egalitarian ideals, value his arduous battles, and recognize his vast metaphysical worldview. The consequence? We are energized to put his message into practice. Through his erudite scholarship and literary sophistication Professor Harbans Singh has succeeded splendidly in offering a balanced, authentic, and inspiring account of the great religious figure of all times. Full attention is given to traditional and scriptural evidence, along with contemporary research. The symbiosis of the historian's objectivity and the devotee's subjectivity is ever alive in Professor Harbans Singh's writing.

The biography contextualizes Guru Gobind Singh as the culmination of the spiritual light, the socio-ethical message, and the very corporeality that began with Guru Nanak and carried through his eight successors. Historians often make a rupture between the "peace-loving" Guru Nanak and the "crusader-warrior" Guru Gobind Singh, which is not only erroneous, but also detrimental to Sikh psyche and society. These *either-or* binaries take away the multi-dimensionality of the Gurus and give a skewed sense of their ideology and praxis. This volume reveals the Tenth Guru as a natural successor to the First who challenged social hegemonies, criticized degrading and exclusive cultural norms, and validated heroism. Guru Nanak's poignant protest against Babur's invasion of India and his devastation of innocent people—both Hindu and Muslim, male and female—resonates throughout Guru Gobind Singh's fight for freedom and justice. In his own voice we hear the Tenth's awareness of his divine purpose: identifying himself with the founder Nanak, he commits to reverse the moral imbalance of his contemporary society, one in which the saints were being persecuted and the tyrants rewarded.

The account captures delightful scenes of the Guru's childhood in Patna where his parents Guru Tegh Bahadur and Mata Gujari were spending some time. Several stories of little Gobind from the *Sri Gur Pratap Suraj Granth* are incorporated here. As we all know stories may not be factual, but they exude enormous power as articulated by Muriel Rukeyser, "the universe is made of stories, not of atoms." The childhood stories portray an enthusiastic, empathetic, wise, loving, and a happy Gobind. The author effectively conveys the youngster's impact: "Its [Patna's] air was intoxicated with the presence of so lovable a being. Its streets echoed with the prattle and mirth of Gobind Singh as he grew up and started ransacking the place with a group of playmates." He would frequently overstay his playtime and return home late which would delay the evening liturgy. Interestingly, even today the tradition is maintained, for the evening Rahiras in the Patna Sahib Gurdwara is still read after the usual canonical hour. In one of the stories, little Gobind announced that he had found a second mother, Rani Maini longing for a child. When Mata Gujari asked how will one son play on two laps, the son responds most poetically: "Just as one moon plays simultaneously in two pools." With his narrative flair, the author delineates a vivid portrait of the Guru, which fosters not only a close relationship with the historical figure but also a deeper understanding of his adult psyche and subsequent accomplishments.

Through his verse the Guru expressed the themes of love and equality, and a strictly ethical and moral code of conduct. Deprecating idolatry and superstitious beliefs and practices, Guru Gobind Singh evoked love for the singular Divine. His quatrains (*savvaye*), for instance, underscore devotion as the basis of religion. They reject all forms of external worship and cast Guru Nanak's message of internal love in undulating rhythm—*"jin prem kio tin hi prabh paio"*(those who love, they are the ones who find the Transcendent). Rather than an impassive list of do-s and don'ts, these poetic rhythms hit us at a visceral level and reproduce spontaneous reactions.

I am glad that Bhai Vir Singh Sahitya Sadan, a premier literary and cultural organization in India's national capital, has decided to reprint this inspirational work on the Tenth Master as a part of 350th birth anniversary celebrations of Guru Gobind Singh, for which I thank its dynamic Director Dr. Mohinder Singh. I also wish to record my gratitude to Dr. Manmohan Singh, Former Prime Minister of India and Sadan's President for his kind Message.

Department of Religious Studies   Nikky Guninder Kaur
Colby College   Crawford Family Professor
Waterville, ME. 04901, USA

Nov. 25, 2016

Contents

CHAPTER - 1

The Heritage

Guru Gobind Singh is nearer to our times than any other of the world's religious teachers and prophets. Not much myth has accumulated around him during the 350 years which part him from our generation. For this reason, he is a better-known historical entity. While this brings deserved attention to his work in the perspective of time and space, the universal nature of his teaching is sometimes not fully comprehended. No image of Guru Gobind Singh will be complete without reference to his spiritual revelation.

In his autobiographical account, *Bachitra Natak* ("The Marvelous Play"), he says that, before he started his earthly journey, his unembodied spirit rejoiced in ethereal bliss. As a result of the devotions practised in an earlier life in the snow-washed solitude of the seven-peaked mountain of Hemkunt, he was able to end duality and had attained identity with the Absolute, dispensing with the necessity of being born again. When the Lord, in His Will, commissioned him to come into the world, he was unwilling to depart the divine presence. Says he:

> Then my wish was not at all to come away,
> For my mind was fastened on the feet of the Lord Almighty.
> But He made known to me His desire.

Thus spoke the Lord:

I bless thee as My son,
And appoint thee to extend the community.
Go and spread *dharma*,
And restrain the world from waywardness.

This is a direct and personal attestation of his prophethood. It is, equally, a testament of theistical values. That God is a reality is clearly witnessed. It is further testified that those who love Him, find Him. Attainable through surrender to His Will and through His grace is complete absorption with the Reality. Also authenticated in the *Bachitra Natak* is the divine descent. The son of God came into the world in fulfilment of ordained purpose—to affirm faith and turn the world from error. Yet Guru Gobind Singh never claimed divinity for himself. To quote again from the *Bachitra Natak*:

Whoever calls me the Supreme Being
Shall suffer in hell.
Recognize me as God's servant only:
Have no doubt whatsoever about this.

He pronounced a curse upon those who should denominate anyone in human form as God. His sovereign pleasure was in being his servant - an instrument for proclaiming His will to the world. He would, he declared, speak unto men as He spoke to him, and not remain silent through any fear of mortals. Nor would he differentiate between man and man on the basis of race or religion. On the equality of men, he always spoke explicitly and emphatically. In his *Akal Ustat* ("In Praise of the Timeless"), he said:

There are Hindus and there are Muslims,
and their many sects.
But recognize all mankind as one.
The Lord is the Creator of all,
Lord the Beneficent, the Bountiful, and the Merciful.
Know no other besides Him!
Worship the One God,
For all men the One Divine Teacher.
All men have the same form,
All men have the same light!

Two hundred years before him, Guru Nanak (1469-1539), founder of the Sikh religion, had preached a similar gospel of love and faith. His simple monotheistic creed supported by a set of humanitarian principles of conduct and presented with an artless humility and conviction of which he alone was capable, made a deep impact on India hollowed by conquest and heavily ritualized religious observances. During his lifetime, Guru Nanak had won a large number of adherents to his teaching. This was the beginning of a new religious fellowship which, in course of time, developed the characteristics of a well-defined community. Guru Gobind Singh wrote in the *Bachitra Natak*, "Guru Nanak established this faith in the Kaliyug and indicated the way to holy men. Sin never troubles those who take to His path."

Guru Nanak's commission came to Guru Gobind Singh through a succession of Gurus, or Prophet-teachers.

What were the essential ingredients of this inheritance? The message of Guru Nanak provided the central tenet. Hinduism and Islam, contestants on the Indian soil for nearly five centuries, found in it a point of concordance. Guru Nanak's mission, sharing some of its teachings with both, had its own transcendent and dynamic character. Its chief doctrine was "the unity of God, brotherhood of man, rejection of caste and the futility of idol worship." He undertook long journeys to spread his message. From the high Himalayas in the north to Ceylon (now Sri Lanka) in the south and from Assam in the east to Mecca and Baghdad in the west, he travelled arduously accompanied by a Muslim companion, Mardana. His simplicity of manner and the universality of his teaching appealed to the hearts of men. A new way of life opened before those who accepted him as their teacher. The repudiation of caste and ritualism was the first distinguishing mark of the newly developing order. Its members now partook of a living faith which led to the crystallization of the true religious spirit and produced a more enthusiastic and vigorous approach to life.

Guru Nanak anticipated the future trends of the evolution of the Sikh movement. Characteristic from this point of view was his criticism of the social reality of his time. Equally meaningful was his reaction to Babar's invasion of India. His heart was deeply anguished and he described the sorrows of Indians - Hindus and Muslims alike - in accents of intense power and suffering. His poems, preserved in the Guru Granth, the Sikh scripture, are charged with intense passion. The literature of that period records no more vehement protest against the foreign invading hordes. Said Guru Nanak:

Leading the wedding-array of sin,
He [Babar] has descended from Kabul
And demands by force the bride, O Lalo.
Gone are the days of Qadis and Brahmans,
Satan himself reads the marriage services, O Lalo.

The Muslim women recite the Qur'an
And in distress remember their God O Lalo.
Similar is the fate of Hindu women,
Of castes high and low, O Lalo.

And again:

God took Khurasan under his wing,
But surrendered India to the invader's wrath.
The Creator takes no blame unto Himself;
It was Death, disguised as the Mughal,
That made war on us.
When there was such slaughter, such groaning,
Didst not Thou, O God, feel pity?
Creator, Thou art the same for all!

Guru Nanak appointed one of his followers, Lahina, as his spiritual inheritor. The latter had so truly imbibed the spirit of Guru Nanak's teachings and impressed everyone so greatly by his piety and nobility of character that the Guru chose him his successor in preference to his own sons. He embraced him and called him "Angad," part and parcel of his own being.

Guru Angad (1504-52) carried forward the work of his predecessor and had the latter's hymns as well as his life-stories written in the Gurmukhi script. This was the beginning of the religious literature of the Sikhs. Guru Angad strengthened the institution of *Guru-ka-Langar*, or community meal for which people sat to eat together, forgetting the distinctions of caste. This served as an instrument of a far-reaching social revolution.

Guru Amar Das (1479-1574) contributed to the growth of the Sikh organization by establishing twenty-two *manjis* (dioceses) covering several parts of India and sought the amelioration of the position of women by deprecating the customs of *purdah* (veil) and *sati* (immolation of a widow on the funeral pyre of her husband). The Fourth Guru, Ram Das (1534-81), founded the town of Amritsar which became the principal seat of Sikhism.

Guru Arjun, Nanak V (1563-1606), was the first martyr of the Sikh faith. He was tortured to death for his religious conviction under the orders of Jahangir. His example generated a new impulse for calm suffering and sacrifice which runs undiluted throughout the course of Sikh history, ennobling and animating a great many of its pages. He also gave Sikhism its scripture, the Holy Granth, and a central place of worship, the Harimandir at Amritsar.

His son, Guru Hargobind (1595-1644) taught the use of arms. Seeing how peaceful resistance to oppression had proved abortive, he recognized recourse to the sword a lawful alternative. Although, no armed conflict took place during the tenure of his successor, Guru Har Rai (1630-61), the discipline the Sikh order had developed was maintained. The Guru kept royal court, with 2,200 horses in attendance. This in no way impeded his spiritual office which was carried out, consistent with the tradition established by Guru Nanak. In fact, the acquisition of strength to repel tyranny and injustice was considered a legitimate religious duty. Sikhism developed this characteristic in the normal course of evolution under the impact of prevailing circumstances.

Guru Har Krishan (1656-64) was a small boy when he assumed the responsibility for leadership and held the charge for a bare three years. Nevertheless, he acted with circumspection and sagacity. What intuitive judgement he brought to the conduct of the community's affairs is evident from his choice of Tegh Bahadur as his successor whom he was able to mention but allusively fi ɔm his sickbed just before he died. He ignored several near relations in choosing Tegh Bahadur, who, though the least desirous of them all, proved to be the most deserving of the honour.

The line of prophetic succession thus came down to Guru Tegh Bahadur (1621-75), father of Guru Gobind Singh. The Sikh character and organization had been used by nine successive teachers, each emphasizing a particular lesson truly exemplified in his own life, or contributing a new national trait rehearsed under the stress of changing times and environment. It was this rarefied and evolved heritage which Guru Gobind Singh came into when he ascended the throne of Guru Nanak.

The Sikhs have always believed that all the Gurus shared the same light and had the same message to impart. They were anointed beings each transferring his light to his successor and delivering to him the holy commission he had inherited. On this, again, the testimony of the *Bachitra Natak* is categorical. Guru Gobind Singh wrote: "Nanak assumed the body of Angad...Afterwards, Nanak was called Amar Das, as one lamp is lit from another...The holy Nanak was revered as Angad. Angad was recognized as Amar Das. And Amar Das became Ram Das...When Ram Das was blended with God, he gave the Guruship to Arjun. Arjun appointed Hargobind in his place and Hargobind gave his seat to Har Rai. Har Krishan, his son, then became Guru. After him came Tegh Bahadur."

CHAPTER - 2

Childhood at Patna

Guru Tegh Bahadur, Nanak IX, assumed the hallowed office at a time when the temporal authority in India had passed into the hands of Emperor Aurangzeb. Aurangzeb took the throne of Delhi expelling his own father, Shah Jahan, who was held captive, in the Fort of Agra. His first few years as Emperor were occupied in consolidating his position, vanquishing his enemies and putting out of his way his brothers one by one. Yet a tour of Guru Tegh Bahadur undertaken in pursuit of his holy mission did not go unnoticed. Accompanied by his family and some of his devoted Sikhs, he was journeying down from Punjab visiting the Sikh *sangats* and proclaiming the message of Guru Nanak. As he was passing through the country near Delhi, reports were made to the Emperor, who distrustful of any collective activity, ordered his arrest. Guru Tegh Bahadur was put under restraint and released only on the intercession of a courtier, Kanwar Ram Singh, son of Mirza Raja Jai Singh of Jaipur, whose family had reverenced the House of Guru Nanak since the time of Guru Hargobind.

Free to resume his travels, he proceeded to the east and visited cities such as Allahabad, Varanasi and Gaya, until he reached Patna. His family could travel no farther. Leaving his wife in the care of her brother, Kirpal Chand, and his own mother, Guru Tegh Bahadur continued his eastward journey to Assam to see places made sacred by the visits of Guru Nanak and to meet his Sikhs.

The ancient city of Patna, which, under the name of Pataliputra, had been the capital of an old Indian kingdom and had remained the chief city of the land for a thousand years, was yet waiting for its moment of crowning glory and blessedness. The place had been sanctified centuries before by the visit of Lord Buddha who had, it is said, come to reprove the founder, King Ajatasatru, for a sin he had committed. On 22 December 1666, a light appeared in one of its simple homes. On that propitious day, Guru Gobind Singh was born to *Mata* Gujari, wife of Guru Tegh Bahadur. Patna was touched with eternal holiness.

Great rejoicing took place at Patna, and, when the happy tidings reached there, at Monghyr, on the Ganga, where Guru Tegh Bahadur then happened to be, a number of his followers and admirers from all over India made a pilgrimage to Patna. Among the very first to arrive was a Muslim *faqir* who, seeing the child, declared him to be a divine being.

In the village of Ghuram, in Punjab, another Muslim saint of much repute and piety, Pir Bhikhan Shah, made, on the day of Guru Gobind Singh's birth, obeisance to the east instead of to the west. At this his disciples demurred, for no Muslim should make such respectful gestures except towards the Ka'ba. The Pir explained that in a city in the east, the Beneficent Lord had revealed Himself through a new-born babe. He had paid homage to the Merciful Lord Himself and to no ordinary mortal.

Gobind Das, the Servant of the Lord, was the name given to the child who became the object of wonder and adoration for many in Patna. In his handsome face haloed by joyous innocence they read the secret of eternity. Patna itself was reborn: it never was to be the old city again. Its air was intoxicated with the presence of so lovable a being.

Its streets echoed with the prattle and mirth of Gobind Singh as he grew up and started ransacking the place with a group of playmates. His most favourite sport was to divide his companions into two sections and enact sham fights. He was always the leader in such games. His toys were imitation bows and arrows and his greatest pleasure consisted in leading his companions through mock-manoeuvres and, then, feast them lavishly in his home at the end of a good day's play. Both his mother and grandmother were greatly delighted to see and entertain his playmates. They gave them sweets and pronounced countless benedictions for them. They rejoiced to see Gobind Singh grow up and were always inwardly praying to Akal to be his protector and keep him away from any harm. As a rule, he overstayed his playtime and returned home late. This delayed the recitation of the *Rahiras*, the evening player. By custom the *Rahiras* in the Patna Sahib Gurdwara is still read after the usual canonical hour.

Another sport Gobind Singh loved was to play tricks on Patna housewives and maidens and break their earthen pitchers with bow-pellets. Not infrequently, complaints were made to *Mata* Gujari. Who can say the victims did not entirely enjoy the fun or that the mother resented having to pacify them and replace the broken earthenware?

For some, a glimpse of the innocent face of the child was a matter of joy. Pandit Shivadat, a revered old Brahman, deeply learned in ancient lore, discovered in it the culmination of a lifetime's quest. He had renounced an aristocratic home in search of inward peace. He turned a devotee, worshipped his chosen idol and practised many austerities. In the city of Patna he was regarded with much esteem for his pious and devout character. Yet he felt he had not found what he had been seeking. There was a sense of emptiness in his heart and he still seemed to be groping for the path until he happened one day to set his eyes on Gobind Singh. A new realization burst forth in his consciousness. He felt he had come to his journey's end. His one desire now was permanently to treasure the gladness that had been conferred on him. This face was now the focus of his meditations and in it he perceived the visions of the deities he had long adored.

A few days later, as Pandit Shivadat sat in contemplation on the bank of the Ganga, his heart filled with his new-found joy, two visitors came to seek of him a favour. They were Raja Fateh Chand Maini and his wife Vishwambhara, popularly known as Rani Maini, who had known him for many years. They had everything that worldly means could procure, but were childless. This caused them much unhappiness. A son was needed in the family not only to inherit their property, but also to perform the prescribed rites at the time of their decease to ensure their passage across the regions of the afterworld. Pandit Shivadat understood the object of their visit and told them that what they sought was within the gift of the heavenly child who dwelt in their own city. He advised them to open the doors of their hearts to him.

Raja Fateh Chand and his wife now had a new object of worship. Their love and yearning grew day by day. Once, as the Rani sat in the courtyard absorbed in her reverie, the young Gobind Singh, out on one of his expeditions with his playmates, entered through the gate tiptoe and, twining his arms around her neck, gently called out, "Mother". The word fell like a sweet melody on her ears and her heart was thrilled. She opened her eyes and was dazed to see Gobind Singh standing in front of her. The miracle she and her husband had been praying for had happened. Both of them were overwhelmed with joy and gratitude. Their craving for a son was ended, and they started spending most of their time in meditation and prayer. Their house became the centre of a Sikh congregation. It has been so since then and is today one of the historic shrines of Patna.

Reaching home, Gobind Singh announced that he had found a second mother.

"Then, how will one son play on two laps?" questioned *Mata* Gujari.

"Just as one moon plays simultaneously in two pools," said Gobind Singh.

Several such stories of Guru Gobind Singh's childhood are narrated in an old Sikh text, *Sri Gur Pratap Suraj Granth*. Here is another. There lived a proud Nawab in Patna. He was the local chief appointed by the kind of Delhi himself. Whenever he rode through the town, he expected every passerby to salute him. Seated upon his elephant, he came one day into the street where Gobind Singh used to play with his friends. The children were attracted by the elephant's jingle bells and collected around the animal out of curiosity. The elephant was caparisoned in velvet and bore costly rings on his tusks. A crowd of people stood respectfully bowing to the Nawab. One of his lackeys turned towards the boys and admonished them to do homage to the Nawab by raising their hands to their foreheads. When Gobind Singh heard this, he said to his band of companions: "Tease and offend the Turk. Grin and grimace at him. He is so haughty." All the children merrily joined in the fun. Much was the Nawab's bafflement and annoyance. But his *mahout* soothed his anger saying, "They are children, sir. They speak out what comes to their lips. They are too innocent to distinguish between the high and the low."

Among the many admirers of Gobind Singh in Patna were two Muslim nobles, Rahim Bakhsh and Karim Bakhsh. They were so much impressed by the piety he radiated that they made to him an offering of two gardens and some land. This property now belongs to the Sikh temple at Patna and is known as Guru-ka-Bagh.

In the midst of this childhood ministry and merriment, Gobind Singh used to long sometimes for the company of his father Guru Tegh Bahadur, whom he had seen but once when he had stopped over at Patna on his way back from Assam. Great was his joy when the word finally arrived for the family to return to Punjab.

CHAPTER 3

Martyrdom of Guru Tegh Bahadur at Delhi

The parting from Patna was not without mixed feelings. All of child Gobind Singh's six years had been spent there and many were the tender associations in his mind of this happy and carefree world. He was excited to see palanquins and *raths* (chariots) being rigged out for the long journey, but he thought at the same time of his associates and playmates. On the day of departure, men and women, Hindus and Muslims, Gobind Singh's young companions, and his devotees, such as Pandit Shivadat, Raja Fateh Chand Maini and his wife, came to considerable distance out of the city, following the emigrating cavalcade. It was a most touching sight when they bade farewell to him, his mother *Mata* Gujari and grandmother *Mata* Nanaki, and sang hymns, wishing them a safe journey.

One perennial consolation for those left behind was the sacred congregation which had taken root in Patna. Morning and evening services were held and the faithful tarried to converse of the fortune that had been theirs until so recently and of the marvelous character of the child prodigy who had been in their midst. The house where Gobind Singh was born was converted into a temple. It is today among the holiest shrines of the Sikhs and one of their five highest seats of ecclesiastical and religious authority called *Takhats* or Thrones. In the temple are preserved some of the relics of the Guru-to-be, such as the cradle, a pair of shoes, arrows and swords and a beautifully calligraphed copy of the Holy Granth he had signed later as Guru and sent to Patna.

The party went by easy stages making prolonged halts at places, such as Varanasi, Ayodhya and Lucknow. The longest halt was at Lakhnaur, near Ambala, in Haryana, where it stopped for more than six months. This was his mother's birthplace, and Gobind Singh spent these months, there very happily. Many Sikhs from the surrounding country came to see him. Among the visitors were two famous Muslim divines, Pir Bhikhan Shah of Ghuram, who had seen him at Patna also, and Pir Arif Din of Kabul.

The entire journey took almost a year to complete. Hearing of Gobind Singh's arrival, people travelled long distances to see him and obtain the fulfilment of their desires. The *masands*, or missionaries of the Sikh faith, led the disciples from their bishoprics to his presence and brought gifts and offerings. The visitors were deeply impressed by his precocity and foretold his greatness as a moral preceptor and hero. Wherever he halted, religious assemblies were held at which the sacred hymns were recited.

At Anandpur, the City of Bliss, he had founded in the foothills of the Sivaliks, Guru Tegh Bahadur awaited his son's arrival. As the party approached the town, the whole populace turned out to receive it. Gobind Singh's entry was hailed with joyous ceremony. Guru Tegh Bahadur thanked the Creator and laid out a repast for whoever would join. As news of Gobind Singh's arrival at Anandpur became known, Sikhs started coming from far and near to pay him homage. They brought him presents of all kinds, including weapons from Kabul and Kandahar and pedigreed horses from Khurasan and Persia. Undoubtedly, Gobind Singh prized the horses more than anything else.

Anandpur was picturesquely set on the spurs of the hills with the high mountain-peak of Naina Devi rising above it about seven miles away. The river Sutlej flowed past, kissing the feet of the hill of Anandpur. This was a sight so much after the heart of Gobind Singh who, in the city of Patna, had fed on the eternal murmur of the Ganga rolling sleepily by. His mind reacted instantaneously to this breathtakingly beautiful and stimulating environment. He roamed the hill and dale freely and his body sucked fresh vigour from the bracing air. Besides the practice of arms and sham fights which he fondly indulged in, he went out following the chase. The daily assemblies under the auspices of his father, Guru Tegh Bahadur, were a source of spiritual inspiration. While at Patna, Gobind Singh had learnt to read Gurmukhi from his mother. His speech had a heavy admixture of the Maghadi dialect of Hindi, and those at Anandpur were both charmed and amused by this mannerism of his. He now began to take lessons in Sanskrit, Hindi and Persian. Sahib Chand Granthi, widely read in classical literature, taught him the former two and Qazi Pir Muhammad the last.

Anandpur was a paradise on earth. For Gobind Singh this was the happiest time of his life. All that one could desire was this. The greatest blessing was the affection of his father, Guru Tegh Bahadur. The mornings and evenings he spent in meditation and in receiving instruction and the rest of the time of day in hunting and other manly sports. At night, before he went to bed in the apartments set aside for him, numerous attendants sang hymns for him from the Sacred Book. But those halcyon days were a prelude to the mighty events and upheavals of which Anandpur itself was to become the epicenter.

The signs of what was coming were, however, not far to seek. A sense of foreboding overhung Anandpur. Guru Tegh Bahadur's sermons daily stressed how *dharma*, or truth, was in jeopardy and what a self-respecting people should do to redeem it. A spirit of daring and resistance was growing. It had its origin in the message of Guru Nanak proclaiming the equality and dignity of man and in the new order he had established to give effect to it. He had a deep awareness of the shortcomings and ills of the Indian society as well as of the abjectness to which it had been reduced. Emancipating the common man from religious and social shackles which had completely devitalized him, and restoring to him his capacity to stand up against injustice and tyranny was the object of his teaching. The process of uplift Guru Nanak had inaugurated received special fillip and acquired new possibilities from the martyrdom that Guru Arjun suffered and the armed resistance his successor, Guru Hargobind, sanctioned, as a last recourse.

With Emperor Aurangzeb's accession to the throne of Delhi, the situation became even more desperate. A pious man in his personal life, he was an orthodox Muslim and cherished the ambition of purging India of the infidels and making it a land "fit for Islam." During his Viceroyalty of Gujarat, he had many Hindu shrines in the province demolished and desecrated the temple of Chintaman in Ahmedabad, finally converting the building into a mosque. He had waded through a river of blood to reach the throne and had imprisoned his father and killed his own brothers. The consciousness of this guilt put a sharper edge of hostility on his religious prejudice and drove him to adopt the harshest measures he could devise against the non-Muslim population. By this policy he wished to please the Muslim orthodoxy and win reprieve for the crimes he had committed to gain the crown. For the first ten years of his reign, he did not feel strong enough to take any drastic steps, but in 1669 he issued a rescript to all provincial governors "to destroy with a willing hand the schools and temples of the infidels and put an entire stop to their religious practices and teaching." Some of the most sacred and important shrines of the Hindus, such as the second temple of Somnath, the Vishwanath temple of Banaras and the Keshavraj temple of Mathura, were destroyed. Among the many repressive edicts issued against the non-Muslims was one prohibiting all Hindus, with the exception of Rajputs from riding *palkis*, elephants or thorough-bred horses and from carrying arms. Most stringent and humiliating was the imposition, in 1679, of the hated *jizyah*, a tax the non-Muslims had to pay for permission to live in an Islamic State. The *jizyah* was a means to replenish the treasure which had been drained by the Emperor's Deccan campaigns and to force those who could not afford to pay to embrace Islam.

The Emperor did not flinch from making forcible conversions. The experiment was first tried in Kashmir. The Kashmiri Pandits were the most literate section of the Hindu population which led the rulers to believe that, if they were brought into the fold of Islam, the task of converting the rest of the people would become easier. The Imperial Viceroy of Kashmir, Iftikhar Khan, carried out the policy vigorously and set about converting the Kashmiris by the sword. To the helpless people pressed by the juggernaut of Mughal persecution, Anandpur promised a hope and thither repaired a group of them in the summer of 1675 to narrate their tale of woe to Guru Tegh Bahadur and seek his intercession.

On their arrival at Anandpur, they represented to the Guru their woes and said that he was the protector of *dharma* by God's dispensation and had the power to help those who came to him in distress. They implored him to preserve the honour of their faith.

As Guru Tegh Bahadur sat pondering over the request that had been made to him, Gobind Singh happened to come along with his playmates. Seeing his father in such a thoughtful mood, he stopped and asked why he looked so deeply preoccupied.

"*Dharma* is at stake," said the Guru. "The oppression of the rulers has reached its limit. Some truly worthy person should come forward to lay down his life to rid the earth of the burden of tyranny."

"None could be worthier than you for such a noble act." remarked Gobind Singh in his innocent manner.

Guru Tegh Bahadur was pleased to hear this brave answer and receive such spontaneous confirmation from his young son, then barely nine, of his wish to sacrifice his life to vindicate human dignity and freedom. He asked his visitors to go and tell the authority in Delhi that, if he (Guru Tegh Bahadur) was converted, they would all voluntarily accept Islam.

Resolved to court execution and thwart the Emperor's plans of making large-scale conversions, Guru Tegh Bahadur set out from Anandpur. He made a prayer to the Lord Almighty to bestow on him the gift of martyrdom, and took leave of his family and his devoted Sikhs.

Earlier, Guru Tegh Bahadur had travelled widely in the territory of Malwa, preaching Guru Nanak's word and exhorting the people to shed fear and be prepared to resist boldly any infringement of their right to belief or of personal freedom. "Frighten none, nor should you be afraid of anybody," was the principle he preached. During these travels, he moved from stage to stage, accompanied by a large number of his followers, receiving homage from the people and their offerings. It was during this tour of the Guru that Muslim followers, such as Saif-ud-Din of Saifabad near present-day Patiala, and the Pathan residents of Garhi, near Samana, served him with devotion.

The imperial news writers had sent to the court coloured reports of Guru Tegh Bahadur's travels. Aurangzeb was now further ruffled to hear of his determination to lay down his life to defend the people's right to practice their faith. He immediately issued orders for his arrest. Soon after leaving Anandpur, Guru Tegh Bahadur was taken into custody on 12 July 1675, at Malikpur Rangharan near Sirhind, and sent to Delhi. He was put in chains and ordered to be tortured until he would accept Islam. Neither physical chastisement nor any worldly allurements had any effect on him. When he could not be persuaded to abandon his faith to save himself from persecution, he was asked to perform some miracle to prove the divinity of his mission. This also he declined, saying that it was never right to try to intervene in the will of God. "God's people would be ashamed of quacks and mountebanks attempting to do this."

Orders for the execution of Guru Tegh Bahadur were received in the beginning of November 1675. His tormentors had given evidence of their cruel intentions by tying Bhai Mati Das, one of his devoted followers, between two pillars and splitting his body into two by sawing it from head downwards. Bhai Dyal Das was thrown into a cauldron of boiling water, and Sati Das burnt alive wrapped in cotton wool. Guru Tegh Bahadur was himself beheaded in public in Chandni Chowk in the afternoon of 11ᵗʰ November 1675. This was an earthshaking event in the history of India. Thus did Guru Gobind Singh write about it in the *Bachitra Natak* :

> He protected their *tilak* and *janeu*;
> In this *kali* age, he performed a grand deed;
> He made the supreme sacrifice for the sake of the men of faith.
> He gave his head,
> but uttered not a groan.
> This martyrdom he endured to uphold righteousness.
> He gave his head, but displayed not his charism.
> Men of God will be ashamed
> To perform tricks like charlatans.
> Casting off his bodily vesture to the suzerain of Delhi,
> He departed to Realms Divine.
> A deed like Tegh Bahadur's none had dared before.
> At the departure of Tegh Bahadur,
> The world was enwrapped in mourning.
> Laments of grief filled the land of the mortals;
> In the sphere of the gods rang shouts of adoration.

The mutilated body of Guru Tegh Bahadur was left in the Chowk unattended and none dared to claim it for fear of the Mughal ire. In the evening there came a storm and it provided Jaita, a Sikh of the humblest caste called Ranghreta, cover to escape with the Guru's head. With his most sacred, but sorrowful, possession, he made his way to Anandpur accomplishing the hazardous journey as fast as he could. The headless body was hidden in a loaded cart by a Lubana merchant, Lakkhi Shah, and carried off to his home. Since open cremation would have amounted to a crime against the State, the Lubana Sikh set fire to his house, burning with it the body of the martyred Guru. The spot is now the site of Gurdwara Rakab Ganj in New Delhi. The place where the Guru was executed is commemorated by another of the Sikhs' holy shrines in the Indian capital, Gurdwara Sis Ganj.

CHAPTER - 4

Remoulding of Spirit at Anandpur

To Anandpur came the dust-laden, severed head of its founder – a sight which must have melted the rocks of the surrounding hills. The mother of Guru Tegh Bahadur, his wife and the Sikhs were overcome by grief. For Gobind Singh, then in his ninth year, it was a tragedy too deep for words. Yet he displayed matchless fortitude and calmness. He first of all greeted Jaita and, embracing him affectionately, paid tribute to his courage and devotion. He exalted his whole tribe by conferring on it the blessing: "*Ranghrete Gur ke bete*" i.e., *Ranghretas* are the Guru's own sons.

He consoled his mother, grandmother and the Sikhs and told them to pray and not to mourn for Guru Tegh Bahadur, who had acted under God's will and set a superb example for the world. There should be no sorrow for the passing of such perfect beings. The Guru, said Gobind Singh, was in the Realm of the Immortals which rang with shouts of adoration for him.

Guru Gobind Singh performed the obsequies with dignity and reverence. "A pyre of sandalwood was constructed and *attar* of roses sprinkled on the head which the young Guru took and solemnly placed on the pyre. He then repeated the preamble of the *Japuji*, the morning prayer of the Sikhs, and ignited the pyre with his own hands. While the head was being cremated, the Sikh congregation sang hymns of the Guru. They called to memory and spoke of Guru Tegh Bahadur's philanthropic and self-sacrificing deeds. The *Sohila*, the last of the Sikhs' five daily prayers, was then read with a concluding benediction and sacred pudding distributed. When Guru Gobind Singh reached home, he caused the reading of the Guru's hymns to be begun, and this was continued for ten days, when alms were freely distributed."

Lakhi Shah and other Sikhs came from Delhi with the sacred ashes. Guru Gobind Singh received them with honour. As he took Lakhi Shah into his embrace, the latter narrated the Delhi events. The entire *sangat* was overwhelmed with emotion. "Hail! Hail!! Guru Tegh Bahadur, *Hind-di-Chadar* (sheet)", i.e. protector of the *Hind*, it proclaimed.

Guru Gobind Singh consoled his Sikhs and bade them not to give way to grief. He said, "My father accepted what was God's will as the course most agreeable. This event will be remembered as long as the sun and the moon continue to shine.

Guru Gobind Singh gradually withdrew Anandpur from the hush that had descended upon it. The hills began to echo with the chanting of the holy hymns and heroic balladry, and with the gallop of the young Guru's noble steed. Martial exercises and sports were resumed with redoubled vigour and hunting expeditions and competitions in horse-racing, musket-shooting and archery became a common feature of life at Anandpur. The Guru's followers were told to bring offerings of weapons and horses, and an endless stream of pilgrims never let the supplies fall behind the daily increasing requirements. Such was the people's zeal for training in the use of arms that a poet, called Hir, who was a contemporary of Guru Gobind Singh, said in one of his verses that a Sikh boy learnt to wield the sword before he learnt to tie his turban. The anguish in the hearts of Sikhs was giving way to a new determination and purpose. It was a new consciousness in birth – a new nation in formation.

On Baisakhi day, 29 March 1676, was held the investiture ceremony when Guru Gobind Singh was formally installed as Guru. The Sikhs came in large numbers from all parts of the country to join the gathering and participate in the ceremonies. The Guru arrived decked in splendid accoutrements and wearing a *kalghi* or plume on his head. The Sikhs were immensely rejoiced to see him looking so handsome and poised. They greeted him with affection and veneration. Hymns from the Holy Granth were sung and a benediction was said before the investiture ceremony. The sacred emblems, which Guru Tegh Bahadur had sent from Delhi before his execution were placed before him as a token of the previous Guru's homage to the succeeding Guru. The *karahprasad*, or the sacramental food, was distributed. For their meals, the Sikhs went to the *Guru-ka-Langar* where they ate together overruling all distinctions and divisions. Guru Gobind Singh had now succeeded to the spiritual sovereignty of the Sikhs as well as to the authority governing their secular affairs.

Another emblem of authority Anandpur acquired was a war drum. Guru Gobind Singh had it especially made, setting aside the advice of some of the *masands* who had said that the beating of the drum would excite the envy of the hill ruler of Bilaspur within whose territory Anandpur was situated. The Guru dismissed it as a feeble argument and said that his equipment would be incomplete without a drum. When ready, the drum was called Ranjit Nagara, the Drum of Victory, and was installed with due ceremony. Everyone was thrilled to hear it beaten powerfully and rhythmically by the strongest Sikh especially chosen for this duty. Usually, the drum was beaten when Guru Gobind Singh went out hunting or at mealtime in the *langar*. The object in the latter case was to make it known that anyone hearing the drum was welcome to join and partake of the food. This is still the custom in all Sikh Gurdwaras.

News of the developments at Anandpur kept pouring into the ears of Raja Bhim Chand of Bilaspur. The deep and thunderous roll of the Ranjit Nagara made him curious and panicky. He called his minister and asked him to find out what the object of the Guru and his Sikhs was in thus disturbing the peace of his country. The minister was a God-fearing and wise man and told the Raja that the Guru meant no harm to him or to his state. He had only come shooting accompanied with the drum he had lately constructed. The minister advised his master to keep on good terms with Guru Gobind Singh and take, as soon as possible, an opportunity to visit him.

This appealed to Raja Bhim Chand and he sent his minister to Anandpur to arrange for the meeting. The Raja's emissary was received by the Guru with courtesy. He was told that his master would be welcome to the Guru's house which was open to all.

Raja Bhim Chand was given an honourable welcome at Anandpur. Guru Gobind Singh engaged him in a long conversation. The second interview took place the following morning in an elegant and costly tent which had been presented to the Guru by Duni Chand, a Sikh from Kabul. Raja Bhim Chand was greatly impressed by the richly embroidered canopy. The sight of the small, but well-trained, elephant, called Prasadi, which was a gift to the Guru from Raja Ratan Rai of Assam, evoked an equally strong admiration in the heart of the visitor. He, however, could not control his jealousy and returned home contemplating on how to dispossess the Guru of those precious belongings.

The wedding of his son, Ajmer Chand, to the daughter of Fateh Shah, Raja of Srinagar (Garhwal), provided Raja Bhim Chand with an excuse and he sent a request to the Guru for lending him the elephant and other articles of display for the occasion. The Guru saw through the design and declined, saying that he could not part with the offerings and presents of his Sikhs. Upon this refusal the Raja wrote to him a threatening letter and said that, if the elephant was not sent, he would obtain his wish by force, march his army against him and eject him from his territory. This also made no impression on the Guru. But Raja Bhim Chand was dissuaded by other hill chieftains from any hasty action. The crisis was averted, though only temporarily, for the Rajput hill monarchs' hostility towards Guru Gobind Singh was deeper than a mere contention over an elephant or a canopy. Besides being jealous of the royal court the Guru kept, they resented the way the four castes mixed in the new brotherhood at Anandpur and the encouragement Guru Gobind Singh gave to the people of, what they called low classes. The Sikh *langar*, where food was shared by all regardless of differences of caste or position, was a challenge to their time-honoured social traditions. They also knew that, after Guru Tegh Bahadur's martyrdom, the Sikhs were no favourites of the Mughal Emperor, and were to be treated as an insubordinate and rebellious group. So they nursed a feeling of disdain and hostility towards them.

In the midst of his engagement with the concerns of the community, Guru Gobind Singh gave his attention to the mastery of physical skills and literary accomplishment. He had grown into a comely youth – spare, lithe of limb and energetic. His limpid eyes reflected the compassion of his heart and the depth of his conviction. His versatility was amazing, and he went through his arduous daily programme with inexhaustible vitality. He rose well before dawn and performed his devotions. He then came to the morning assembly where he listened to the sacred hymns being sung by the musicians and gave expositions of the scriptural texts. The rest of the day was spent in recitations of heroic poetry, drills and athletic competitions and in ministering to the needs of the disciples. The evening assembly was followed by common board and discourses far into the night.

As a result of his assiduous training and practice, Guru Gobind Singh gained unique facility in the use of arms. None could match his skills at swordsmanship and archery, nor had he an equal as a horseman. He displayed similar prowess at learning. Besides Punjabi, he gained proficiency in Braj, Sanskrit and Persian, and acquired extensive knowledge of ancient lore. He had a natural genius for poetic composition. The total volume of his compositions would fill a lifetime of exclusive dedication to the Muse. He bore a highly artistic and elegant hand at Gurmukhi calligraphy, specimens of which are fortunately preserved on the leaves of some copies of the Holy book of his time

and in the form of his "signatures' on several of his
hukamnamahs or letters which have come down to us.

The *Var Sri Bhagauti Ji Ki*, popularly called *Chandi-di-Var*, written in 1684, was his first composition and his
only major work in Punjabi language. Few poems in
Punjabi literature equal *Chandi-di-Var* in virility of tone
and structure. The poem depicts the titanic contest
between the gods and the demons. Its magnificent martial
cadences and vivid imagery aptly recapture the sounds and
fury of a battle-scene. The emphasis is on the image of
Goddess Durga which, through the poetic imagination and
fervour of its creator, attains reality and firmness belying
its mythical origin. Such is the impact of this poem that
people in Punjab have a superstition and will be chary of
reciting it first thing in the morning, lest it should arouse
them to warlike action. But the Nihangs and others
heroically inclined read it regularly and derive much
inspiration from it.

Guru Gobind Singh had chosen the *Puranic* story of
Durga's valorous fight against the demons with a view to
infusing new spirit into his people. His narrative follows
in the main the original source, the *Markandeya Purana*,
but a dominant interest of the poem lies in the character
of Durga, which has been drawn with poetic insight.

The eight-armed Durga, so the story goes, was born
of Vishnu. When Brahma, attacked by a demon, Madhya
Kaintabha, wiped off perspiration from his forehead into
the ocean, another demon, Jallandhara, sprang to life from
the drops. Pursued by the demons, Brahma sought shelter
with Vishnu who was then sitting in deep meditation. As
Madhya Kaintabha advanced towards Vishnu, out came
Durga splitting open the latter's side to fight the demons.

She was brave and handsome. Thus is she described by Guru
Gobind Singh in his Hindi poem, *Chandi Charitra* :

> Luminous like the moon is her face, and a sight of
> it charms away many a woe.
> Her hair hangs like Shivaji's serpents, her eyes
> are the envy of both lotus and the gazelle.
> Her brows are in the manner of a bow;
> her lashes like the arrows.
> She has the waist of a lion and marches with
> the majesty of a royal tusker.
> She abides on the mountain-top; none can
> resist the splendour of her charms.
> She holds a sword in her hand and rides a lion;
> Flaming like gold is her presence.
> In another hand she carries a bow of war.
> The fish are shamed by her restless energy;
> The lotus and the gazelle by the softness of
> her eyes;
> The parrots by her nose;
> The pigeons by her neck;
> The cuckoo by her voice;
> The pomegranate by the pearly row of her teeth.
> Lighting upon the person of the goddess,
> The moonbeams have become more lustrous
> than before.

The story, in Punjabi poem *Chandi-di-Var*, by Guru
Gobind Singh, begins with the demons overthrowing the
gods and establishing their own sway where the gods once
ruled. The Satyuga, the age of truth, is past and it is now
the time of the not-so-true Treta. Great discord prevails
in the world; Narada – famous for his ability to stir up
discords and passions – is abroad.

The gods in their helplessness turn to Mount Kailash where Durga lives. Their leader, King Indra, supplicates the goddess for help : "Thy shelter we seek, goddess Durgshah!" Riding her demon-devouring lion, Durga at once sets out to annihilate the evil-doers.

A fierce battle ensues, and the heavens are torn by the beating of drums, blowing of shells and the piercing cries of war. The sun becomes invisible in the dazzling brilliance of shiny swords and spears.

In the awesome confusion of battle, the long-haired heroes fall to the ground, in agony, like drunken madmen. Those pierced with spears lie motionless like olives on the branch of a tree. The fallen warriors look like so many domes and turrets struck down by lightning. The demons fight with dreadful determination and not one of them has been seen fleeing the field. Their womenfolk watch the bloody scene from their towers, amazed at the goddess's wondrous valour.

Durga's sword seems dancing in her hand raining death on the dauntless foe. The demons, full of wrath, close in upon her roaring like the black clouds. The mighty Mahkhasur arrives in great fury. But Durga smites him with such force that her sword, breaking the helmet to pieces and piercing through the body of the rider, the horse and the earth, rests on the horns of the bull (who supports the earth). The Queen, upon her stately lion, tears through the battle-ranks of the demons demolishing them with her deathly sword. "Durga, by God's grace, has won the day." Restoring to the gods their lost kingdom, she returns.

Another battle takes place later and Guru Gobind Singh describes it in equally vivid and vigorous Punjabi verse. The chief point of *Chandi-di-Var* lives in its martial feeling which is evoked by a succession of eloquent similes and a dignified, echoic music of the richest timbre. The poem, though not the size of a true epic, has a remarkable breadth of sweep and intensity and a heightening rhythmical tempo with well-marked climactic patterns. On the reader's mind it has a most stirring and invigorating effect. The production of this kind of heroic literature was one of the means used for the uplift of the spirit of men. Anandpur had become a seat for unique experimentation in recasting the human soul.

Among the batch of Sikhs who came to Anandpur from Multan for Baisakhi celebrations in 1682 was the gifted and accomplished young man, named Nand Lal Goya. He was a scholar of Persian and Arabic, and wrote poetry in the former language. His ancestors had been ministers at the court of Ghazni, and he had inherited from them their love of Persian letters. He presented Guru Gobind Singh with one of his Persian works entitled *Bandagi Namah*, the Book of Worship. The Guru was pleased with this gift and complimented Bhai Nand Lal. Looking through the book, the Guru suggested that it should be called *Zindagi Namah*, the Book of Life. The book has since been known by this title.

At the age of 17, Guru Gobind Singh was married to Sundari, daughter of Bhikhia, a resident of Lahore. Unmindful of the custom, he refused to go to Lahore for the wedding. He founded instead a small town near Anandpur and called it Guru-ka-Lahore. His disciples and followers thronged the place. Bhikhia came with his family, and the nuptial ceremonies were performed amidst much jubilation.

The following year came in a party of new converts, a Sikh who had a daughter, called Jito, of marriageable age. He proposed to the Guru to wed her, but he did not desire the alliance. It was, however, pressed on him by his mother and the nuptials were solemnized soon afterwards. Jitoji died in 1701. The same year, a Sikh from Rohtas, Harbhagwan by name, offered him the hand of his daughter, Sahib Devan. As her parents insisted and she herself prayed that she did not want anything except to be allowed to remain with him to serve him, the Guru agreed. She was later declared mother of the Khalsa, as manifested by Guru Gobind Singh.

Guru Gobind Singh had four sons. Ajit Singh was born to *Mata* Sundari on 26 January 1687. His other three sons were born to *Mata* Jitoji, Jujhar Singh on 14 March 1691, Zorawar Singh on 17 November 1696, and Fateh Singh on 25 February 1699.

CHAPTER - 5

A New Literary Metaphor

Raja Medini Prakash of Sirmur was one among the hill rulers who did not support Raja Bhim Chand in his designs against Guru Gobind Singh. He wished to invite the Guru to spend some time with him at Nahan which had a cool climate and abounded in game. This was conceived to assuage Raja Bhim Chand's temper and to enhance his own prestige, especially to impress his rival, Raja Fateh shah of Srinagar. He sent his envoy to Anandpur, but the Guru could not immediately say if he would be able to go to Nahan and asked the messenger to wait a few days for the answer. Some of the *masands* were keen that he should accept the invitation and leave Anandpur temporarily. They spoke to the Guru's mother, and on her advice, he decided to visit Raja Medini Prakash.

He left an adequate guard at Anandpur and, beating the big drum, Ranjit Nagara, to proclaim his departure, he set out towards Nahan, accompanied by his relations and a body of trained Sikhs. He halted at Kiratpur where he visited the shrine of his grandfather, Guru Hargobind. When he reached the vicinity of Nahan (14 April 1685), the Raja came out to greet him and considered himself fortunate in having him as his guest. He took him to his palace and looked after him and his Sikhs in a most hospitable manner.

It was not the intention of Guru Gobind Singh to stay as the Raja's guest for long. While out in pursuit of chase one day, he was immensely taken up with the natural scenery of a spot on the margin of the Jamuna. The place was within his host's territory, twenty-six miles from Nahan, and the Guru immediately set up camp there. After making a prayer to the Supreme Lord and distributing the customary sacred food, he laid the foundation, on 29 April 1685, of a fortress on which his Sikhs and the Raja's men worked diligently day and night. The building was soon ready and he took up his abode in it. The Guru named the place Paonta, from the *pav* or foot of his horse implanted on this soil when it had instantly attracted his heart.

The years spent at Paonta were the most creative and significant in Guru Gobind Singh's career. The activities which filled his days at Anandpur were revived here and he gave a considerable part of his time to the religious and martial training of his followers. He engaged himself in his favourite outdoor pastimes and, as he says in the *Bachitra Natak*, he "slew in the forest of this place many tigers, bears and antelopes." But here he also contemplated deeply and long on the state of the country and here it was that his grand design for recovery and renovation took shape in his mind. His poetic intuition and energy found exuberant expression and he created verse which is incomparable for its sublimity of style, mystical ardour and virility of content. His object was two-fold - to sing praises of the Timeless and to infuse new vigour into a weak and emaciated mass of people. His compositions were most appropriately adapted to these purposes. Rarely has poetry in any language recaptured the transcendent vision in such personal and realistic terms or inspired such a spirit of courage and heroism.

In this poetry, Guru Gobind Singh created a new metaphor – the metaphor of the sword. The sword was the symbol of *Shakti*, *Kalika* or Durga and of Akal Himself. God was described as '*Sarbloh*', or All-Steel. This symbol was intended to give a new orientation to the thinking of the people, demoralized and debilitated by subjugation to foreign rule and the streak of passivity in their very nature. They needed a new vocabulary and a new principle of faith. This, Guru Gobind provided by coining the new figure. At the beginning of the *Bachitra Natak*, he says:

> I bow with love and devotion to the holy sword.
> Assist me that I may complete this work.
> God and sword are mentioned here synonymously.

Then follows a ringing and soulfully rendered invocation to the sword. The diction, a form of Prakrit, is so powerful and it reproduces the clangorous rhythm of clashing swords with such verve that the verses may be quoted in the original:

> *Khag khand bihandang, Khal dal khandang,*
> *Att runn mandang, Barr bandang.*
> *Bhujj dandd akhandang, Tej parchandang,*
> *Jot amandang, Bhann prabhang.*
> *Sukh santa karnang, Durmatt darnang,*
> *Kilbikh harnang, Ass sarnang.*
> *Jai, jai jag kaaran, Sristt ubaaran,*
> *Mamm pratipaaran, Jai tegang.*

Thou art the Subduer of Kingdoms, the Destroyer of the armies of the wicked.

In the battlefield Thou adornest the brave.
Thy arm is infrangible, Thy brightness ɪ efulgent,
Thy radiance and splendour dazzle like the sun.
Thou bestowest happiness on the good.
Thou terrifiest the evil, Thou scatterest sinners.
I seek Thy protection.
Hail! hail to the Creator of the World,
The Saviour of creation, my Cherisher,
Hail to Thee, O Sword!

God and Sword became interchangeable terms. The preamble to the Sikh *Ardas*, or supplication, which is of Guru Gobind Singh's composition, begins with the words: "Having first remembered the Sword, meditate on Guru Nanak..."

When he referred to God as *Sarbloh*, or Sword, the Guru was not oblivious of His characteristics of love and compassion. A couplet in his *Jap Sahib*, remarkable for its description of the divine attributes, says:

I bow to Thee, Lord, Who art the wielder of the sword!
I bow to Thee, Lord, Who art the possessor of arms!
I bow to Thee, Lord, Who knowest the ultimate secret!
I bow to Thee, Lord, who lovest the world like a mother!

God is symbolized in the weapons of war. He is presented as the Punisher of the Evil and the Destroyer of the Tyrant. The benevolent aspect is simultaneously and equally forcefully emphasized and He is invoked as the Fountainhead of Mercy, the Kinsman of the Poor and the Bestower of Felicity. This fusion of the devotional and the martial, of the spiritual and the heroic was the most important feature of the teaching of Guru Gobind Singh and of his career as a spiritual leader and harbinger of a revolutionary impulse.

At Paonta it was his custom to go out after the morning's meditation and assembly and walk along the Jamuna far enough to locate a spot which appealed to his heart for its beauty and solitude. He would then sit down and compose poetry uninterrupted for three hours. Sometimes these creative reveries lasted much longer. Once when he was composing the *Akal Ustat* he went into such a rapturous trance over the word *tuhi*, or 'Thou Alone', that he sat in this state for sixteen hours. Sixteen times the word *tuhi* was repeated in that verse in the hymn.

First of all, he completed the story *Krishanavtar* which he had commenced at Anandpur. Likewise, he took up several other themes from ancient epics and mythology to produce verse charged with martial fervour. This reference to the very sources of Indian culture was the result of a happy poetic instinct. About his purpose Guru Gobind Singh left no one in doubt. Writing a finis to *Krishanavatar*, he said:

I have cast into the popular tongue the story of Bhagvat.

This I have done with no other purpose, Lord, except to glorify the holy war.

A brave death in battlefield for a holy and religious cause was set out as a noble and worthy end. In one of the hymns, Guru Gobind Singh supplicates God in the following manner:

Grant unto me this boon, O Lord,
That I may never be deterred from doing good deeds.

I should have no fear of the enemy
When I go to battle,
And turn victory assuredly to my side.
In my mind there is but one desire
That I may ever be singing Thy praises.
And, when the time comes, I should die
Fighting in the thick of action.

This was the literary image that had been developed at Paonta, and the emotional ethos it had created.

In this way Paonta became the centre of a spiritual and cultural regeneration. For its quantity alone, the literary production of Guru Gobind Singh's years at Paonta was very significant. Besides his own compositions which were copious, there were the contributions of the courtly bards. Hearing of the reputation Paonta enjoyed as a seat of poetry, many devotees of the Muse had flocked to the Guru's court. Fifty-two of them were in his permanent employ. Among them were Saina Pat, Lakhan, Kanshi Ram, Ani Rai and Sukhdev. To break the exclusive monopoly of the priestly class in the field of learning and literary composition, Guru Gobind Singh sent five of his Sikhs to Banaras to study Sanskrit. They were the founders of the Nirmala School of letters among of Sikhs. Learning no longer remained the preserve of the high-born. One day, Guru Gobind Singh surprised a learned Brahman by having an ornate and esoteric couplet of his interpreted by a simple-looking Sikh returning from his chores in the community kitchen.

Apart from singing panegyrics to their preceptor, the court poets wrote on a variety of subjects such as love, mirth, pity, anger, heroism, terror and wonder, and made translations from the old Sanskrit texts. They were rewarded generously for their labours. The Guru presented a poet, named Hans, sixty thousand *takas* for translating the 'Karna Parva' of the *Mahabharata*. A vast mass of literature in Braj and Punjabi languages was produced in this manner. The work was subsequently continued at Anandpur. These compositions comprised a huge volume named *Vidyasagar* or *Vidyasar*. Guru Gobind Singh greatly valued this book. This priceless treasure was washed away in the flooded stream of Sirsa at the time of the Guru's evacuation from Anandpur after a prolonged battle with the Mughals and hill rajas. No one can guess the extent of loss thus caused to Indian literature.

Guru Gobind Singh's compositions are preserved in the *Dasam Granth*, the Book of the Tenth Master, as distinguished from the *Adi Granth*, the Original Book, which is the scriptural text. Two of these, the *Jap Sahib* and the *Sudha Sawwaiye*, are among the daily prayers of the Sikhs. The former, in nearly 200 verses and employing ten different metrical measures, is full of ennobling and stately hymns in praise of God. It is pure of sentiment and design. The wealth of its verbal innovation and imagery and the cascading music of its rapidly changing vigorous and recitative metres make a deeply lyrical impression on the reader's mind. The *Akal Ustat* and the *Sabda Hazare* are two other songs of divine praise. The *Sastra Nam Mala* lists the weapons of war with much mythological narration and symbolic meaning. The *Gian Prabodh Granth* is, in part, a lesson in practical philosophy conveyed through metaphysical discussion. Marvellous deeds of the twenty-four incarnations of Vishnu are described in the *Chaubis Avatar*, whereas the *Chandi Charitra* and the *Var Sri Bhagauti Ji Ki* resurrect the Puranic legend of Chandi.

All of Guru Gobind Singh's works reveal the power of his poetic imagination and his mystical intuition. They show also the amazing range of his learning and knowledge in the fields of mythology, metaphysics, astronomy, human psychology, geography, botany, Ayurveda and warfare. He had a command of several languages such as Braj, Arabic, Persian and Punjabi. His compositions were mostly in Braj which then enjoyed vogue as the language of literary expression. In Punjabi, his major work was the *Var Sri Bhagauti Ji Ki*. He possessed an uncanny mastery over the magic of words and used them with natural ease to render a variety of moods, scenes and sounds. There was the harmony of the spheres in his verse as well as the irresistible flow of hill rivulets and the graceful sweep of a galloping steed. He adopted many traditional moulds and measures, but his own prosodic innovations were prodigious. Likewise, he created myriads of original images and similes to lend embellishment and meaning to his verse. For its loftiness of tone, resonant timbre and opulence of symbolism, Guru Gobind Singh's poetry remains unmatched. It inspired vast numbers of people and revivified and enriched the Indian literary tradition.

Poetry as such was not for him an end in itself. It was a means of revealing to the world the divine principle and of concretizing the personal vision of the Supreme Being that had been vouchsafed to him. Through his poetry he preached love and compassion and a strictly ethical and moral code of conduct. He preached the worship of the One Supreme Being, deprecating idolatry and superstitious beliefs and observances. The glorification of the sword itself was to secure fulfilment of God's justice. The sword was never a symbol of aggression and it was never used for self-aggrandizement. It stood for righteous and brave action for the preservation of truth and virtue. It was the emblem of manliness and self-respect and was to be used only in self-defence, as a last resort. For Guru Gobind Singh said:

> When all other means have failed,
> It is but righteous to put the sword in hand.

CHAPTER - 6

Victory by Akal's Favour

The tranquil, poesy-laden atmosphere of Paonta was disturbed by an unnecessary conflict forced upon Guru Gobind Singh. Emperor Aurangzeb was too far away, occupied with his south Indian campaigns, to take much notice of affairs in the North, but his feudal vassals, the hill chiefs, had always resented the Guru's teachings and his presence in their midst. While returning from the wedding of Raja Bhim Chand's son to the daughter of Raja Fateh Shah of Srinagar, they plotted together to make an attack on Paonta. For the Guru, it was a mystery why they should have done so: in the *Bachitra Natak*, he said that Raja Fateh Shah "raged and fought with me purposelessly." He had, in fact, brought about accommodation between Fateh Shah and his rival, the Raja of Sirmur, and had sent presents on the occasion of his daughter's marriage. These he returned under pressure from his son-in-law's father, Raja Bhim Chand, and joined the attacking host.

Guru Gobind Singh met the army six miles from Paonta at a place called Bhangani. Before the battle started, five hundred of his Pathan soldiers broke loyalty with him and went over to the rajas. They had been demobbed from the Mughal army and commended to the Guru's favour by Pir Buddhu Shah, a Muslim divine of Sadhaura, who was himself a follower. These men were engaged and kept at Paonta. The *Udasis* who had come with the Guru from Anandpur also fled before the battle commenced. Only their leader, Mahant Kirpal Das, remained to atone for their faint-heartedness by his deeds of valour. To make up for the desertion of the Pathan mercenaries, Pir Buddhu Shah was on hand with his four sons and seven hundred of his followers. Then there were the Guru's Sikhs – not professional soldiers, but men imbued with the spirit of heroism and eager to sacrifice their lives for the Guru. By their brave actions, they more than met the taunt of the Pathans who, when deserting, had said that it would be fun seeing the Guru's untrained rabble fight in their absence.

The spot Guru Gobind Singh had selected was between the Jamuna and its tributary, the Giri. It gave him advantage in strategy and its choice was proof of his knowledge of the tactics of war. His five stalwart cousins – Sango Shah, Jit Mal, Gopal Chand, Ganga Ram and Mahri Chand – each led a section of troops. The battle raged fiercely as the two armies faced each other.

The Pathans fought with unusual venom and fury and one of their leaders, Hayat Khan, caused much damage in the ranks of the Sikhs. Armed with a heavy club, Mahant Kirpal Das came forward to challenge him. The Pathan scorned fighting a priest armed merely with a staff, but, challenged twice, he rushed forward and dealt him a heavy blow with his sword. The Mahant received it on his club. Then rising in his stirrups and shouting *Sat Sri Akal* vociferously, he struck Hayat Khan's head with his wooden truncheon so mightily that his skull was crushed. The scene was described by Guru Gobind Singh in the *Bachitra Natak* in a vivid simile. He wrote: "Mahant Kirpal, raging, lifted his club and struck the fierce Hayat Khan on the head, upon which his brains spilt forth as butter flowed from the Gopis' pitchers broken by Lord Krishna." The account is further continued: "Nand Chand raged in dreadful, ire, launching his spear, and then wielding his scimitar. When the keen weapon broke, he drew forth his dagger for the honour of the Sodhi race. Then my maternal uncle, Kirpal, advanced in a rage. The brave man's body received many arrows, yet he emptied the saddles of many a Pathan horse. Sahib Chand, as a true warrior, strove in the battle's fury and slew bloodthirsty heroes. Many excellent warriors were slain and those who survived fled with their lives. Sango Shah, Lord of Battle, gloriously acquitted himself and trampled underfoot the fierce Pathans." The Guru also paid tribute to the gallantry of Hari Chand, one of the hill rajas. "The brave Hari Chand planted his feet firmly on the field and, in his fury, discharged sharp arrows which went through and through his adversaries."

One of the Guru's cousins, Jit Mal, fell in single combat with Hari Chand. Sango Shah and his adversary, the Pathan leader Nijabat Khan, were both killed in the combat they engaged in. Then Guru Gobind Singh mounted his charger and rode into the thick of the contest. He confronted Hari Chand, and the action which ensued is thus described in the *Bachitra Natak*: "Hari Chand, in his rage, drew forth his arrows. He struck my steed with one and then discharged another at me, but God preserved me and it only grazed my ear in its flight. His third arrow penetrated the buckle of my waist-belt and reached my body, but wounded me not. As I felt the touch of the arrow, my wrath was aroused. I took up my bow and began to discharge arrows. Upon this my adversaries began to flee. I took aim and discharged an arrow. The young chief, Hari

Chand, was killed...The hillmen fled in consternation. The victory was mine, through Thy favour, Akal!"

The Guru blessed Sango Shah, Jit Mal and his other brave Sikhs. He especially praised the devotion of Pir Buddhu Shah, who had fought in the battle on his side and whose two sons were killed in action. The wounded on both sides were given the help they needed and those slain were disposed of according to the ordinances of their faiths.

Guru Gobind Singh's Sikhs, unused to the way of war, surpassed their trained and professional adversaries in courage and dexterity. This gave them confidence in their arms and the neighbouring mountain monarchs learnt to respect their power. The battle at Bhangani took place on 18 September 1688. Soon thereafter the Guru left for Anandpur.

While at Paonta, Guru Gobind Singh had a very touching meeting with Baba Ram Rai, son of Gur Har Rai, Nanak VII, who lived in Dehra Dun on the other side of the Jamuna. He had garbled a verse from the Holy Granth to please Emperor Aurangzeb and was, for this sin, debarred from succession to Guruship. He thus fell out of the mainstream of Sikh History. But he was a gifted man credited with miraculous powers. He had a considerable following of his own and had a large estate in the Dehra valley given him by the Mughal Emperor who was one of his admirers.

When Baba Ram Rai heard of his uncle, Guru Gobind Singh, being so close to where he lived, he became desirous to see him. He sent a messenger to Paonta and a day was fixed for both of them to meet on the bank of the Jamuna. Baba Ram Rai, who was meeting the Guru for the first time, greeted him with reverence and both had a long and cordial converse. The *masands* of Baba Ram Rai who had accompanied him felt embittered to see this scene of family reconciliation.

Guru Gobind Singh was still at Paonta when Baba Ram Rai died on 4th September 1687. He made a trip to Dehra Dun to condole with his widow, Punjab Kaur. She complained of the highhandedness and corruption of her husband's *masands* and besought him to restrain and chastise them. The guru invited the *masands* to meet him. He charged them with dishonesty and frivolity and punished them according to their crime. The honest and pious among them were rewarded.

The departure of Guru Gobind Singh for Anandpur created a puzzling situation for the Raja of Sirmur. He wished to call on him and offer his tribute before he left his territory, but was afraid of his kinsmen. He had remained neutral in the hostilities they had started against the Guru. To go to him and do him the honours of state at the time of farewell would have given them serious offence. The Guru saved him the embarrassment by making a sudden departure.

He marched by way of Sadhaura. He had chosen this route especially to meet his devotee, Pir Buddhu Shah, who lived at that place. At Raipur, the Guru was hospitably received by the local Rani, who sought his blessing for her son. He said that the young boy should grow his hair long and gain skill in the use of arms. Before leaving, he presented the boy with a sword and shield. As the Guru proceeded to Anandpur, many people had their desires fulfilled by seeing him in person and receiving the sacred message he had to deliver.

Anandpur had been depopulated in Guru Gobind Singh's absence and had to be rehabilitated. With his arrival, the Sikhs started pouring in and many of them settled there. The town once again throbbed with the inspiration that had made it the centre of a vital spiritual rebirth before the Guru's departure for Paonta. The old tempo of life was revived and the currents arising from it spread out to wider areas in the country.

In order to fortify the town, Guru Gobind Singh constructed four forts on strategic hill features, and called them Anandgarh, Lohgarh, Kesgarh and Fatehgarh, respectively. The first-named was the largest, with a lofty battlement around it and with water reservoirs and stores inside.

What was being preached at Anandpur gradually had its influence on the hill people also. Encouraged by the presence to the Guru among them and taking advantage of Aurangzeb's continued involvement in the South, some of the hill chiefs stopped paying tribute to the Mughal government. Mian Khan, the Viceroy of Jammu, despatched his commander, Alif Khan, to bring the recalcitrant princes to book. Raja Kirpal of Kangra and Raja Dyal of Bijharwal submitted without resistance and told the chief of the punitive force that, if he subdued the Raja of Bilaspur, he should obtain the surrender of all the hill people. They themselves joined hands with Alif Khan to fight him.

The Raja of Bilaspur had already made his peace with Guru Gobind Singh by paying him a visit on his return to Anandpur. He now solicited his assistance against the Mughal commander. The Guru himself turned out with a body of his chosen Sikhs. Alif Khan was forestalled at Nadaun, on the left bank of the Beas, twenty miles south-east of Kangra. The battle, fought on 20 March 1691, was quick and decisive. Guru Gobind Singh described it in the *Bachitra Natak* in vividly cadenced and rousing verse. "Then," said he, "the Almighty God hastened the end of the fight and the opposing host was driven away into the river." Alif Khan fled in utter disarray "without having the chance to care for his camp."

The news of the discomfiture of the expedition sent by his officer reached Aurangzeb. He felt irritated by the reports he had received about the growing influence of Guru Gobind Singh and his part in defeating Alif Khan's force. The Emperor immediately ordered his *faujdars* in Punjab to restrain the Guru from holding assemblies of Sikhs and to demolish his hearth and home and banish him from the country if he departed ever so little from the ways of a faqir and did not cease to have himself addressed by his Sikhs as *Sacha Padshah*, the 'True King'. The imperial edict, which was issued in November 1693, caused no dismay at Anandpur, nor did it depress the spirit which had been kindled there. Guru Gobind Singh sent out instructions, asking his Sikhs to assemble in large numbers at Anandpur on the occasion of Baisakhi and come armed, with locks and beards unshorn.

Sikhs came from all parts of the country as bidden by the Guru. In addition to the normal hazards of travel, they encountered at places hostile Mughal columns. They fought wherever anyone tried to harass them and reached the city of Guru Gobind Singh which was their destination. The festival of Baisakhi was celebrated on 29 March 1694, with religious assemblies, chanting of the sacred hymns, community meals and competitions in sports and martial exercises. Reports of this Sikh concourse were sent to Aurangzeb in the Deccan by his news writers.

The next imperial expedition was directed mainly against Guru Gobind Singh. The Mughal chief, Dilawar Khan, sent his son with a strong force to defeat him and then turn his attention to the hill rulers. The young commander, marching with alacrity, reached the vicinity of Anandpur at midnight and intended to surprise the town. The Guru wrote in the *Bachitra Natak* that, as the troops crossed the river, his chamberlain Alam Chand, awoke him. The word went round and the Sikhs arose and, putting on their armour, rushed out to meet the invaders. The beating of the Ranjit Nagara and the zestful and stentorian war-cries of the Sikhs echoed widely in the stillness of the dark winter's night, giving an exaggerated impression of their numbers. The Mughal force was completely unnerved at the suddenness of the Sikhs' movement, and beat a hasty retreat without giving battle. "The Khan fled shamelessly, without using his weapons. The mighty heroes ran deserting the battlefield," wrote Guru Gobind Singh in the *Bachitra Natak*.

Dilawar Khan fell into a rage on hearing of this disaster. While his son stood in front of him with his head sunk low, his commander, Husain Khan, offered to go and avenge the defeat on Guru Gobind Singh. He proceeded towards Anandpur with a larger army at the beginning of 1696. Several hill chiefs submitted to him. Among them was Raja Ajmer Chand of Bilaspur, whose father, Raja Bhim Chand, along with Guru Gobind Singh, had measured swords with Alif Khan.

Husain Khan was diverted from his progress towards Anandpur by his involvement with Raja Gopal of Guler. The latter could not produce the heavy tribute levied upon him and prepared himself for an armed conflict. He was aided by his ally, Raja Ram Singh of Jaswan. Sangatia and seven other Sikhs who had come as an embassy of peace to the court of the Guler chief also took part in the battle. Husain Khan was supported by the rajas of Kangra and Bilaspur. In the fierce action (20 February 1696) that ensued, both Husain Khan and Kirpal Chand of Kangra were slain, and the Raja of Guler and his allies won a decisive victory. Sangatia and his seven Sikhs fell fighting the Mughals in this bloody battle. The Raja of Guler celebrated the triumph by presenting offerings to the Guru and rendering him gratitude for his help. Dilawar Khan sent out yet another expedition against Guru Gobind Singh. But this was also doomed to failure like its predecessors. Before it reached Anandpur, the force was challenged by Gaj Singh of Jaswan at Bhalan. Its leader, Jujhar Singh, was killed in the contest which sealed the fate of the venture.

These repeated disasters made the Emperor desperate and angry. On 13 July 1696, he sent his eldest son Muazzam, who later succeeded him to the throne of Delhi as Emperor Bahadur Shah, to settle affairs in Punjab. The prince stationed himself in Lahore and sent one of his officers, Mirza Beg, towards the Sivalik hills. Mirza Beg brought the rajas to their knees and wreaked a cruel vengeance. Guru Gobind Singh was, however, left alone. The reason was the intercession made by Bhai Nand Lal, a devoted Sikh of the Guru, who was a member of Prince Muazzam's *entourage*.

Still the pressure of Mirza Beg's operations was felt in Anandpur. Guru Gobind Singh in his *hukamnamahs*, addressed to his followers, enjoined upon them to come with weapons of war and horses. One such letter written in August 1696 to Tiloka and Rama, ancestors of the Phulkian rulers, is still in the possession of its present scion, Captain Amarinder Singh of Patiala. In this letter, Guru Gobind Singh called their house his own and asked them to come to him with their horsemen. This was repeated, in very urgent terms, more than once.

CHAPTER - 7

The Moment of Creation

For some time there was no threat either from the Mughals or the Rajput rajas and Guru Gobind Singh betook himself to poetry and reflection during the intermission. He spent the time in seclusion at the foot of the lofty hill of Naina Devi, not far from Anandpur. Here he completed in 1698 the *Bachitra Natak*, a versified account of his own life. His poets made translations from the *Upanishads* and other classics, such as *Hitopades* and *Chanakyaniti*. In this state of constant communion and elevation, the Guru discerned how eventful the coming years would be. He finalized his scheme of redemption which had been maturing in his mind for some time, and prepared to bring his mission to its ordained consummation.

A preparatory measure he undertook was the reformation of the Sikh ecclesiastical organization. The *masands*, who were supposed to be the leaders of Sikh congregations in various parts of the country and enjoyed the status of the Guru's own representatives, had become neglectful of their religious office and were corrupt and oppressive. The Guru had heard many complaints of how they exploited his innocent and devoted Sikhs. As intermediaries between the Guru and the local *sangats* or communities they took advantage of their position for personal aggrandizement and flayed their flocks mercilessly. Their counsel was always one of caution and timidity, and they attempted to subvert the Guru's daring and resistance.

Once a party of wandering minstrels came to Anandpur and performed in the presence of the Guru and his Sikhs. One of their most amusing and telling satires was on the *masands* whose actions were depicted with much sarcasm and persiflage. The Guru had determined to abolish this order which was oppressing the people and undermining the Sikh structure. He summoned the *masands* to come to Anandpur and divested them of their positions. Those of them who had serious charges of misconduct to answer were punished and a few who were good and honest were honoured by him. The system was abolished once for all and the *sangats*, freed from the excesses and tyranny of *masands*, were now directly linked with Anandpur.

Baisakhi at Anandpur had always been an occasion for fervid celebrations and reunion of the followers and disciples from the remotest parts. For the festival in 1699, Guru Gobind Singh had ordered special preparations to be made. Messages were issued to the Sikhs to come in full strength, wearing arms and maintaining their beards and hair inviolate. Elaborate arrangements were made at Anandpur for the reception of the pilgrims. The Guru remained absorbed for long intervals and the Sikhs noticed on his face the reflections of his deep meditations and in his eyes a strangely far-away look. He seemed to be occupied with an unfathomable inner wonder and mystery. The air in Anandpur was tense with anticipation. Everyone went about his work slightly subdued by the self-consciousness of the moment. Stillness prevailed where there used to be so much of energetic fun and gaiety –

a stillness which prefigured momentous events.

As Baisakhi approached, Anandpur started humming with the pouring streams of visitors. Chroniclers record eighty thousand persons to have assembled for the occasion. On the day of the festival (March 30), Guru Gobind Singh, as usual, rose early and sat in meditation. He then donned his uniform and arms and appeared before the assembled Sikhs. Instead of starting his sermon which the disciples had been waiting to hear, he unsheathed his sword, and, addressing the vast congregation, said "My sword wants today a head. Let any one of my true Sikhs come forward. Isn't there a Sikh of mine who would sacrifice his life for his Guru?"

His words numbed the audience. They did not know what the Guru meant and gazed in awed silence until he spoke again. Now confusion turned into fear. For the third time, the Guru reiterated his call. Daya Ram, a Khatri of Lahore, arose and said with humility, "My head is at thy disposal, my True Lord. There could be no greater gain than dying under thy sword." He walked behind the Guru to a tent nearby. The Guru returned with his sword dripping blood and demanded another head. This was more than many could endure. People started leaving the place. Some of them went to complain to the Guru's mother. But Dharam Das, a Jat of Hastinapur, stood up and said with folded hands, "Thy humble servant offers himself, Great Lord! He had consecrated his head to thee, True King, when he became thy Sikh." Guru Gobind Singh made three more calls. Mohkam Chand of Dwarka, Himmat of Jagannath, and Sahib Chand of Bidar cheerfully responded one after another and advanced to offer their heads.

After a while, Guru Gobind Singh led the five Sikhs

back from the tent into which he had taken them one by one. In that tent, erected on a hillock and confidentially guarded, he had kept dresses especially made for the occasion. Decked in saffron clothing topped over with neatly tied turbans of the same colour, the Glorious Five walked deferentially behind their Master, overwhelmed with thankfulness. The Master was himself attired in the same manner as his chosen disciples. The assembly, considerably thinned and still in shocked muteness, was further puzzled to see those whom they had thought to have been sacrificed to the Guru's whim return in flesh and blood.

The Guru introduced his companions to the audience as *Panj Piare*, the five devoted spirits beloved of the Guru. He gave vent to his feelings of immense gratefulness to Akalpurkh for the fulfilment which had crowned Guru Nanak's teaching. He said that, by coming through the supreme test immaculately, the Beloved Five had blessed themselves and brought glory to their faith. They would, added Guru Gobind Singh, form the nucleus of the order of the Khalsa, God's Own, he was going to inaugurate.

He then proceeded to hold the ceremony of baptism. Filling an iron bowl with clean water, he kept churning it with a two-edged sword while reciting over it the sacred verses. *Mata* Jitoji came with sugar crystals which were put into the vessel at the Guru's bidding. Sweetness was thus mingled with the alchemy of iron. The *amrit*, or Nectar of Immortality, was now ready.

The Guru gave the five Sikhs each five palmsful of it to drink. The disciple sat *bir-asan*, i.e. in the heroic posture, with the left knee up and the right knee to the ground. Every time the Master poured the nectar into his palm, he called out aloud: *Wahiguru ji ka Khalsa, Wahiguru ji ki Fateh* (Hail to the Khalsa who belongs to the Lord! Hail to the Lord to Whom belongs the victory!!). The Sikh repeated the blessed utterance. After the five life-giving draughts had been administered, the Master sprinkled the holy liquid into his face gazing intently into his eyes kindling his spirit with his own inner light. He then anointed his hair with the nectar consecrating it, eternally to the Lord. At the end, all five of them were given the steel bowl to quaff from it turn by turn the remaining elixir in token of their new fraternal comradeship. Their rebirth into this brotherhood meant the annihilation of their previous family ties (*kul nas*), of the occupations which had hitherto determined their place in society (*krit nas*), of their earlier beliefs and creeds and of the ritual they had so far observed. Their worship was now to be addressed to none except Akal, the Peerless and the Timeless One. Their father was Guru Gobind Singh and their place of birth Anandpur. The moment marked a complete break with the past.

The five Sikhs – three of them so-called *Shudras* or outcastes a *Kshatriya* and a *Jat* – formed the nucleus of the self-abnegating, martial and casteless fellowship of the Khalsa Guru Gobind Singh had brought into being. They were given the surname of *Singh*, meaning lion, and were ever to wear the five emblems of the Khalsa – the *kesha*, or long hair and beard; *kangha*, a comb tucked into the *kesha* to keep it tidy in contrast to the recluses who kept it matted in token of their having renounced the world; *kara*, a steel bracelet; *kachha*, short breeches worn by the soldiers of that time, and *kirpan*, a sword. They were enjoyed to succour the helpless and fight the oppressor, to have faith in One God and to consider all human beings equal, irrespective of caste and religion. Thus did Guru Gobind Singh speak to them: "You are the sons of Guru Nanak, the Creator's own, the chosen ones. I name ye the Khalsa. Ye are the disciples of the Word, and ye shall be the saviours of man. Ye shall own no property and ye shall love man as man, making no distinction of caste or creed. Ye shall keep forever this flame of life lit in you, unflickering, in deep meditation on the One Timeless Being. Ye shall bow your heads to your Master only. Ye shall never worship stock, stone, idol or tomb. Remember always in times of danger or difficulty the holy names of the masters, Nanak, Angad, Amar Das, Ram Das, Arjun Dev, Hargobind Sahib, Har Rai Sahib, Har Krishan, Tegh Bahadur. I make ye a rosary of these names; and ye shall not pray each for himself, but all for the whole Khalsa. In each of you the whole brotherhood shall be incarnated. Ye are my sons, both in flesh and spirit."

Guru Gobind Singh asked the five initiated Sikhs to prepare the *amrit* as he had done. When it was ready, he stood before them with folded hands and besought them to baptize him into their brotherhood. This sounded to the disciples as a strange request, but he explained by telling them that the order of the Khalsa had been created under the direct command of Akal. The Guru must be one of them, for there was to be no difference between him and the Khalsa. He had created the Khalsa in his own image. The Khalsa was his embodiment, his alter ego and his much beloved ideal (*isht suhird*). "As Guru Nanak seated Guru Angad on the throne, so have I made the Khalsa Guru," said Guru Gobind Singh.

The Guru had always held his Sikhs in high esteem and spoken of them in terms of appreciation and deference.

According to the *Khalsa Mahima*, he said:

I have won my battles through the favour of my Sikhs;
Through their favour have I been able to dispense largesse.

Through their favour my troubles have receded,
And through their favour my prosperity expanded.
It is through their favour that I acquired knowledge;
Through their favour I subdued my enemies.
Through their favour am I exalted;
There are, else, millions of such humble persons as myself.
Let my body, my mind, my head, my wealth, and all that is mine,
Be dedicated to their service.

The five Sikhs, now invested with authority as the Khalsa, stirred water and sugar-puffs to holiness in the manner sanctified by the Master. Then he sat in front of his disciples in the posture he had himself set – his left knee up and his right knee to the ground, and went through the ceremony of initiation, shouting, repeatedly, after them the newly coined greetings: *Wahiguru ji ka Khalsa, Wahiguru ji ki Fateh.* "Hail," as the poet subsequently sang, "to Gobind Singh who is himself master as well as disciple." On being baptized by his own disciples, his name was changed from Gobind Das to Gobind Singh. In this process, he had merged himself into the Khalsa and endowed it with the charisma of his own personality.

Guru Gobind Singh then spoke to all the Sikhs present. He said, "I wish you all to embrace one creed and follow one path obliterating all differences. Let the four Hindu castes which have different rules for their guidance, abandon them altogether, adopt the one form of adoration and become brothers. Let no one deem himself superior to another. Let men of the four castes receive my baptism, eat out of one dish and feel no disgust or contempt for one another." He told the audience that it was not an easy path to choose. It was the path of faith and sacrifice and of strictly moral personal ethics and rectitude. He invited such of the Sikhs as were prepared to abide by the discipline and principles enunciated to come forward and receive the baptism and the insignia of the Khalsa order.

To quote from a report of the proceedings; "Though several refused to accept the Guru's dispensation, about twenty thousand men stood up and promised to obey him, as they had the fullest faith in his divine mission." The novitiates came forward in batches to receive the baptism. The first five among those who now volunteered were Ram Singh, Deva Singh, Tahal Singh, Ishar Singh and Fateh Singh. They were called by the Guru *Panj Mukte*, or the Five Liberated Ones. Countless batches followed, one more eager than another. Anandpur, was seized with an uncanny fervour of the spirit. Baptismal ceremonies continued for several days and thousands of Sikhs entered the fold of the Khalsa, renewing themselves in body as well as in soul.

Further injunctions were laid down for the Sikhs. They must never cut or trim their hair and beards, nor smoke tobacco. A Sikh must not think of another woman, except his own wife, nor should he eat the flesh of an animal killed slowly in the Muslim way. Violation of any of these rules meant his excommunication from the Khalsa. To return to the fold, he must be rebaptized, pay a fine which could mean rendering personal service in the community kitchen or cleaning the shoes of the *sangat* assembled in religious prayer and pledge himself not to repeat the offence. The

Sikhs were forbidden to have anything to do with those who worshipped images, killed their daughters or countenanced *sati*. The Sikhs were asked to eat regardless of caste with those who had been baptized and deem them their brothers, to assist one another in time of need, to live by the toil of their hands never begging for charity, and to contribute a tenth part of their earnings for the common purposes of the community. They were not to covet another's property or money offered in the name of religion. Religious offerings were especially taboo for the Sikhs and Guru Gobind Singh often used to quote to them the following verse of Bhai Gurdas, a learned and pious Sikh of the time of Guru Arjun:

As is the custom of Hindus to abstain from the flesh of the kine,

As swine and interest are forbidden the Muhammadans,

As a father-in-law is prohibited from drinking even water in his son-in-law's house,

As a sweeper, though hungry, will not eat hare's flesh,

As a fly gaineth no advantage but dieth in the clasp of honey,

So is greed for sacred offerings which are like poison coated with sugar.

A living faith in One Immortal God was presented as the central principle which gave meaning to human existence and to all activity. Guru Gobind Singh bade his Sikhs to invoke His blessing by prayer before starting upon any work or enterprise.

The inauguration of the Khalsa was the realization of Guru Gobind Singh's divinely inspired vision and of his design for the uplift of the people. It was a grand creative deed of history which wrought a revolutionary change in men's minds and aroused their dormant energies to positive and altruistic purposes. They were made conscious of the disabilities of their state, of their servitude and abjectness and taught to stand up on their feet and work ceaselessly and courageously to redeem their predicament. They were rid of the superstitions and divisions which had enfeebled and entombed their spirits for centuries and were given a new conceit of themselves and their destiny. A new impulse of chivalry arose in northern India which resulted in an endless chain of shining acts of bold sacrifice and gallantry giving an irrevocable and decisive turn to the course of events.

How Guru Gobind Singh shook out of their passivity a people reconciled for long to their fallen state, their will to action completely atrophied, is one of the miracles of history. To his invitation to join the new order he had initiated to fight oppression, the hill rajas had replied, "Each Turk can eat a whole goat. How can we, who eat only rice, cope with such strong men? Can sparrows kill hawks, or jackals devour tigers?" This psyche of defeat and surrender, not peculiar to the hill rajas alone, had to be superseded. By the alchemy of his *amrit*, the baptismal nectar, and all the metaphysics which culminated in this regenerative principle, Guru Gobind Singh touched the people with faith and courage. He made one Sikh equal to "125 Thousands" and had "hawks" killed by "sparrows." Ordinary human beings – suppressed and ostracized, who had never touched a sword and would have cowered at the sight of blood – were turned into stout-hearted warriors. Thus Guru Gobind Singh transfused life into the limp and languid body of India.

His followers had been given leonine appearance by

the external insignia of their faith. The enlargement of the soul gradually led to bodily amplitude. The Sikh warriors of the eighteenth and nineteenth centuries were as mighty of deed as they were of limb. Jassa Singh Ahluwalia, Nawab Kapur Singh, Baba Ala Singh, Hari Singh Nalwa, Akali Phula Singh, Sham Singh Attariwala and Maharaja Sher Singh, to name but a few, who by their personal heroism left a deep impress on the events of their times, were tall and handsome men, cast in huge moulds, picturesque and broad-chested.

The Khalsa, as consummated by Guru Gobind Singh, was the climax of the 230 years of spiritual and social awakening since Guru Nanak. In the Khalsa came to fruition its basic impulse. The process of evolution continued through the lives of the ten Gurus gaining momentum from the direction each of them provided and from the pressure of contemporary events. The faith founded by Guru Nanak became a political force. Yet, it involved no departure from the essential tenets preached by him. In fact, all the elements of Khalsa discipline were traceable to the doctrines sanctioned by Guru Gobind Singh's predecessors. The central point in the system he had created was belief in One God. This was the foundation of the Sikh faith and Guru Gobind Singh's entire life and poetic utterance provided the sublimest vindication of this principle. Individual piety was never the sole end of Guru Nanak's religion. Amelioration of man in relation to society was its main object. Guru Nanak himself had vigorously protested against idolatry, superstitious dogma and caste tyranny and set himself to remedy these ills. He had protested against foreign invasion and the injustice and cruelty of the rulers of the day. Over the years, the

Sikh community had developed as a compact fellowship around the personality of the Guru. The Gurus had always given it precedence over themselves. "If the Guru counted for twenty, the *sangat* counted for twenty-one." This *sangat*, an assembly of the devotees liberated from caste restrictions and religious formalism and ready always to do the Guru's bidding, became the nucleus of the Khalsa commonwealth. Even the warlike cult emphasized by Guru Gobind Singh was no innovation introduced by him. Guru Hargobind, Nanak VI, had chosen himself a warrior's equipment for the ceremonies of succession instead of the rosary and other saintly emblems and had put on two swords, declaring one to be the symbol of his spiritual and the other that of his temporal investiture. The spiritual and the temporal, the religious and the martial mixed in the Khalsa commonwealth brought to fulfilment by Guru Gobind Singh as an instrument of God for the advancement of humanity. The sword was the emblem of the Khalsa, but, if he carried the weapon in one hand, the other hand was meant to finger the rosary.

CHAPTER - 8

Sparrows Kill the Hawks

Guru Gobind Singh was now thirty-three, and at the height of his mental and physical powers. His influence grew day by day. He commanded the adoration and allegiance of an ever-expanding body of disciples and followers. By bringing forth the Khalsa in circumstances, dramatic as well as mystical, and by establishing with it an intimate personal identity, he completely and inalienably annexed the minds and imaginations of the people of his mission and created an active and viable force to crusade for its fulfilment. He was the object of the affections of a well-knit and zealous community. To do his bidding was considered by everyone the rarest of privileges and to die for him a merit to be devoutly cherished.

The Sikhs returned from the Baisakhi at Anandpur to their homes kindled with fresh enthusiasm and charged with the task of administering baptism to those who were ready to receive it. According to the custom established by Guru Gobind Singh any five initiated Sikhs could preside over the ceremony and administer *amrit* with attendant rites and injunctions. This confirmed the principle that the Guru was representatively present wherever any five Sikhs assembled for a religious purpose. The Sikhs coming from Anandpur related with zest and joy the unforgettable and transforming experience they had passed through and spoke proudly of the insignia of their new life. Many were excited to hear their stories and decided to go and have themselves similarly endowed. A large number of seekers came to Anandpur now than ever before.

People of all classes and castes came, especially those who had been depressed and despoiled for generations under an obstinate social system. They could now discard the stamp of inferiority and attain equality with the highest in the land. Equally, if not more, enthusiastic were Punjabi peasants who found in Guru Gobind Singh a leader completely after their hearts – strong, chivalrous and daring. Robust and hardy yeomen, having been through history's many vicissitudes as the frontiersmen of India, they were ever ready to beat the ploughshares into swords. The Guru's message promised them action and liberation and struck a deeply responsive chord in their hearts. Their minds had been fertilized by the teachings of the earlier Gurus, and the seed now sown by the Tenth Master could not have fallen on a more productive soil. A large number of them turned out to be initiated into the sacrament of the double-edged sword. Channelizing and taming the warlike strain of such virile people to creative ends and charging it with saintly idealism was as great a miracle of the Sikh religion as arming the castaways of Indian society and other non-martial people and making them vehicles of a formidable revolution and of some of the staunchest deeds of sacrifice and heroism in the annals of mankind.

Anandpur throbbed with the new rhythm the establishment of the Khalsa had set. The arrival of every new party of Sikhs gave a thrill to the inhabitants and the ceremonies of baptism were conducted amidst scenes of fraternal joy. The novitiate and the initiated, the newly arrived and the old inhabitants, the disciples and the Master shared alike this emotional experience. The ties that were forged at Anandpur created a society which was free and united and democratically constituted. Caste and origin were totally obliterated. It was now one common spiritual parentage (father: Guru Gobind Singh) and one domicile (Anandpur) for all. It was a fellowship of men and women imbued with the highest idealism and philanthropy – a microcosm of a universal human brotherhood. There were no classifications and distinctions of any kind, nor any privilege. There was no educational hierarchy, no priests or bishops. Even the Guru's army was without any categorized ranks. The Master himself was without any categorized ranks. The Master himself was one of the commonwealth, having been admitted to it like any of the disciples. He observed the same rules as were applicable to them. Once while out hunting, he seemed to make obeisance to a tomb. The Sikh questioned him and said that this was contrary to the doctrines of their faith. The Guru felt pleased to have been checked thus and admitted the Sikhs' sense of propriety and bold confidence.

Everything at Anandpur belonged jointly to the Khalsa. No one had any personal property. All ate from the common Guru-ka-Langar. Everyone contributed his share of labour or service in one form or another. The bulk of the Sikhs came from the working classes, the real salt of the earth. The Guru was happier in their midst than anywhere else. To repeat a commonly quoted story, he once asked for a glass of water. The son of a wealthy merchant, who had come to pay homage to the Guru, went and brought a tumbler which he presented to him decorously. The Guru admired the promptness of the young man, but said that his hands were too delicate and he had not yet learnt to use them for manual work. He must not, he said, drink water from such soft hands.

Devotion to the Guru and a spirit of elation were the dominant notes of life at Anandpur. The Guru was the beloved of all hearts, the object of universal admiration and praise. He was the source of inspiration and strength and the instrument of benignity and compassion. He was the ideal in manly bearing, courage and stamina. With him on their side, the Khalsa felt they could dare death itself and vanquish the mightiest of hosts. This was the prevailing mood at Anandpur – the mood of faith, confidence and optimism. One Sikh announced himself as an army of a lakh and a quarter. A new chivalric vocabulary developed in this style, especially in the days of ruthless persecution which later overtook the Sikhs. In this *patois*, limitations and adversities were made light of and described in a high-spirited language of challenge and bravado, and articles of worldly comfort and glory belittled to the point of ridicule. Death was called an expedition of the Khalsa into the next world. A man with empty stomach would call himself mad with prosperity. He who was making a meal of gram out of necessity would describe himself as eating almonds. Onions were silver pieces, rupees pebbles, and a club the repository of wisdom.

The ripples of this *elan* and of the will to freedom which the Khalsa symbolized spread out to vaster areas. The stirrings of a new movement began to be felt, especially in Punjab. Anandpur became the Mecca for those whose hearts rebelled against the inequality and tyranny of the rulers; it was also the asylum for those who besought safety from their persecutors. Among such persons were two distinguished poets, Kuvresh and Bhai Nand Lal. The former was the son of the famous Hindi poet, Keshav Das of Bundhelkhand. Refusing to be converted to Islam, he fled to take refuge with the Guru. On arrival, he presented to him a petition in verse. The Guru accepted it happily, and agreed to keep him at Anandpur on a generous reward. Bhai Nand Lal was native to Anandpur, being a Sikh of the Guru and having visited the place as a youth. He had subsequently taken up service with Prince Muazzam, the eldest son of Aurangzeb. He possessed great command of the Persian language and once, when several of the courtiers were asked to compose a reply to a missive received from the King of Persia, his draft was deemed the most suitable and selected for despatch. The Emperor thought that such a learned man should not be allowed to remain a Hindu and desired that he should be converted. When Nand Lal came to know of his intention, he resolved to flee to Anandpur. He confided the secret to one of his Muhammadan friends, Ghyassudin, who was a high official. The latter also offered to accompany him to Anandpur to place himself under the Guru's spiritual guidance. Both of them escaped and reached Anandpur where they were received by Guru Gobind Singh with much courtesy.

Bhai Nand Lal, pseudonym Goya, wrote several books in Persian verse, e.g. *Zindagi Nama, Tausif-o-Sana, Ganj Nama, Jot Bikas* and *Diwan-i-Goya*. His writings, like those of Bhai Gurdas, a learned and pious Sikh of the time of the Fifth Nanak, rank only next to the scriptural texts of the Sikhs and can be recited in Sikh *Gurdwaras* along with the Guru's hymns. His descriptions of Guru Gobind Singh are highly evocative, and his compliments to him are saturated with deep love and reverence.

Another happy reunion was with some of the Sikhs from Patna. The Guru was very happy to learn that Fateh Chand Maini and his wife, and Pandit Shivadat whom he had known since his childhood would be visiting Anandpur. He came out to receive the party. He hid himself as the palanquins came in sight and, getting behind them, whooped loudly – a prank he had often tried on Pandit Shivadat as he sat on riverbank enwrapped in meditation. The pilgrims first took fright, but gave way to unbelievable joy as soon as they learnt who had come out to surprise and receive them. They were completely overcome by emotion and tears rolled down their cheeks. Mixed with their happiness was a feeling of pride at seeing their child-idol grow into such a handsome and dignified youth. The Guru entertained them at Anandpur for several weeks and there was during that period much nostalgic remembrance of days gone by.

During these years, Guru Gobind Singh had nothing more to do with the surrounding hill rajas than to invite them once to embrace the Khalsa faith. This invitation they had summarily declined for fear of their Mughal overloads, and more especially, owing to their age-old caste scruples. However, the Guru bore them no grudge and continued to live on terms of amity with them. But they were inwardly burning with envy and waiting for the opportunity when they could restart their offensive and extinguish forever the menace they thought was developing at Anandpur. Two of them, Balia Chand and Alam Chand, once finding the Guru hunting in the valley with only a few attendants, made an assault. The Sikhs fought back courageously and badly mauled the attackers. Balia Chand was killed and Alam Chand lost one of his arms.

This incident made the hill chiefs even more

apprehensive and they decided to apply forthwith to the Mughal authority for help. The Emperor wa. then in the Deccan. So a petition was sent to his Subadar in Delhi. The rajas complained: "Knowing that Guru Gobind Singh was successor of the holy Guru Nanak, we made no objection to his residence among us. When he obtained power and we essayed to restrain him, he went to Nahan and there formed an alliance with its raja. He then came into collision with Raja Fateh Shah of Srinagar, which ultimately led to the battle of Bhangani, where there was great destruction of human life. After his return to Anandpur, the Guru established a new sect distinct from the Hindus and the Muhammadans, to which he has given the name of Khalsa. He has united the four castes into one, and made many followers. He invited us to join him and promised, if we consented, that we should obtain empire in this world and salvation in the next. He suggested to us that, if we rose in rebellion against the Emperor, he would assist us with all his forces, because the Emperor had killed his father, and he desired to avenge his death. As we did not think it proper to oppose the Emperor, the Guru is displeased with us, and now gives us every form of annoyance. We cannot restrain him, and have accordingly come to crave the protection of this just government against him. If the government considers us its subjects, we pray for its assistance to expel the Guru from Anandpur. Should you delay to punish and restrain him, his next expedition will be against the capital of your Empire."

The rajas' representation was forwarded to the Emperor and in due course, two of the Panjhazari Mughal commanders, Painda Khan and Din Beg, were sent out to bring the Guru to book. At Ropar, the hill rajas joined them with their contingents. The Guru descended the hill of

Anandpur to meet the oncoming army. In the arrangements he made, the five Sikhs who had responded to his call on the Baisakhi day and were the first to take the baptism were given important commands. The battle was fought on the banks of a small stream on 26 June 1700. The Sikhs fought with skill and courage. Seeing them so determined, Painda Khan shouted to his men to intensify the attack and earn divine pleasure by winning the holy war and killing the infidels. But no amount of pressure could dislodge the Sikhs from their position. Painda Khan now challenged Guru Gobind Singh to single combat to decide the issue and asked him to attack first lest he should regret afterwards. The Guru said that he would never strike except in self-defence and invited Painda Khan to deliver the first blow.

Painda Khan took two chances and discharged two arrows at the Guru one after the other. The first one sizzled past his turban, and the second one missed him equally narrowly. It was now the Guru's turn. Painda Khan was encased in armour from head to foot, yet the Guru's arrow caught him fatally in a vulnerable spot near his ear and he fell off his horse prone on the ground. The end of Painda Khan made his troops furious, and they set on the Sikhs with redoubled venom. But the Sikhs stood their ground firmly and caused further havoc in the ranks of the adversary. Foreseeing the outcome of the contest, the rajas took to flight. Din Beg could continue the battle no longer. The Sikhs pursued the fleeing force as far as Khizrabad, where a shrine now commemorates this triumph of theirs. They could have gone farther, but the Guru restrained them and said that it was not proper to chase the fugitives. He was gratified to see his Sikhs stand with such firmness in battle's array and rendered a prayer of thankfulness on returning to Anandpur.

The hill rajas nursed their mortification and continued plotting against the Guru. Ajmer Chand who had succeeded his father, Bhim Chand, as the Raja of Bilaspur was chosen as their envoy to go to the Emperor to seek again his assistance and costly presents were collected to be offered to him on their behalf. But before Ajmer Chand could start on his journey, Bhup Chand of Handur, an impetuous youth, insisted on launching an attack. He said it was no use waiting until help arrived from Delhi or Lahore. Each day wasted mean further accretions to the Guru's following and the consequent additional strength to him. If they acted unitedly, they could still beat the Sikhs. He concluded his address by saying: "A reed is a frail support, but a handful of reeds bound together are not easily broken. If we all join together, the Sikhs will be powerless to offer us resistance."

Bhup Chand had spoken with such passion that the proposal for despatching an envoy to the imperial court was given up, and preparations for another attack on Anandpur started. The rajas of Jammu, Nurpur, Mandi, Kulu, Keonthal, Guler, Chamba, Srinagar, Dadhwal, and others came with their forces and, making a rapid march, reached the outskirts of Anandpur. Their plan this time was to invest the town and insulate it from contact with the outside world.

Before opening the attack, Ajmer Chand sent a letter to the Guru to surrender, pay rent for the land on which Anandpur was built and undertake to pay it regularly thereafter. If he was not disposed to accept these terms, he must prepare for his departure from Anandpur or take the consequences.

The Guru sent a suitable reply, saying that his father

had purchased the land and paid for it. Any further payment they could have at the point of the spear alone. He asked them to abandon their pride and then take from him whatever they desired. The Guru's house, he said, was open to all and invited them to make their peace with the Khalsa. He offered to act as a mediator.

But the rajas had come with the intent of destroying the sect, and were in no mood to listen to any counsel of conciliation. Anandpur was reinforced by the timely arrival of 500 Sikhs from Majha under the leadership of Gurbakhsh Singh, Kalal Singh Bharowal and Duni Chand, grandson of Bhai Salo, a distinguished Sikh who lived in the time of the Fourth and Fifth Gurus. Sher Singh and Nahar Singh were entrusted with the defence of the Fort of Lohgarh and Ude Singh with that of Fatehgarh. Weapons such as bows and arrows, *teghs* (cutlasses), *katars* (small daggers), *jamdhars* (two-edged dirks), s*arohis* (flexible swords), *sangs* (pikes), lances, *bichhuas* (daggers, literally, scorpions), scimitars, *selas* (spears) and muskets were distributed among the Sikhs. Meanwhile, the armies of the hill rulers tightened their siege of Anandpur.

The siege lasted many days, but without much effect. Sikhs made bold sorties by night, causing damage in the opponents' camp and carrying away their supplies. The assaults made by the rajas' troops to break the fortifications were beaten off with considerable loss. In the attacks that the Sikhs made, Ajit Singh, Guru Gobind Singh's eldest son, then barely 14, won praise for his feats of skill and valour. As a last resort, the hillmen advanced to attack in full force, headed by a huge drunken elephant, clad in steel armour. The target was the Fort of Lohgarh and they had planned to use the elephant for battering the formidable gate down. Guru Gobind Singh sent out Bachittar Singh, one of Bhai Mani Singh's ten sons, to check the elephant. Bachittar Singh, happy in his heart for having been chosen by the Guru for the task, made a powerful thrust with his spear piercing the plate and injuring the elephant in the forehead. The animal ran back in panic and trampled underfoot several of the hill soldiers. In the open battle that ensued, both sides suffered heavy losses, but the army of the allies was crippled by the deaths of Kesari Chand of Jaswan and Jagatullah, leader of the Gujjar and Ranghar tribes, and by severe injuries to Raja Ghamand Chand of Kangra and the Raja of Handur. Ultimately, the rajas' forces were compelled to raise the siege and flee for safety.

The Raja of Bilaspur was seething with bitter rage at the ignominy he had repeatedly suffered. He made yet another desperate attempt, this time with the help of the *faujdars* of Sirhind and Lahore. The combined troops marched on Anandpur. The Guru came out to meet them at Nirmoh close by. A quick battle took place on 8th October 1700, in which both armies fought desperately. For a while, the allies seemed to be getting the better of the contest. But the Sikhs rallied and launched a vigorous onslaught. The allies were thrown back. The Guru himself moved on to Basali. The raja of that place had always been friendly to him and had invited him to come and stay in his territory. But here also he was allowed no repose. The Raja of Bilaspur followed him with his troops. But the Sikhs inflicted another severe defeat on him forcing him to retreat. In this action fell Sahib Singh, a valiant fighter who had distinguished himself in all the battles in which he had taken part. The Guru returned to Anandpur and to peace, however short-lived.

CHAPTER - 9

Anandpur Evacuated

Whatever peaceful interval Guru Gobind Singh was permitted was devoted to the religious instruction of the Sikhs. Soldiering was not their occupation, nor their aim. None of the actions they had so far engaged in were of their seeking, and they had sought neither communal glory nor territorial acquisition from their victories. The sources of Sikhs' inspiration lay deeper and these the Guru constantly replenished by reminding them of the essentially spiritual and humanitarian basis of their origin. The warlike cult had been reared or the endorsement of these principles, and its subservience to the over-riding moral law was never disregarded.

The Guru now had the opportunity of reviewing the state of the baptized Sikhs. He felt satisfied to see that they had maintained the highest standards of chivalry in battle and had not swerved from loyalty to their Guru or to their faith in the most difficult of situations. They did not give way to despair in defeat, nor lost their humility in victory. The Guru used to cite the example of Alam Singh, who, after baptism, had renounced not only his pride of birth but also the profession of his forefathers. He had taken to arms as if he were a soldier born and made himself the hero of many a battle.

The Guru said that a Sikh who wore his hair long but

did not care to be baptized would never please him. Similarly, Sikhs who worshipped cemeteries and tombs, gods or *pirs* and went to fortune-tellers to have their future foretold should never attain merit. A Sikh might receive an offering of money for making a copy of the Holy Book or for reading it, but he should feed with it the poor before feeding himself. A Sikh might receive instruction from another Sikh, irrespective of his high or low position. He who called himself a true Sikh of the Guru, should accept baptism and perform good acts. One of the Guru's favourite sayings was that, so long as the Sikhs retained their distinctive entity in deed and form, they should continue to enjoy power and influence.

Raja Ajmer Chand of Bilaspur, who, like his father, Bhim Chand, was a prodigal of overtures for amity as of breaching treaties solemnly made, sent friendly messages to Guru Gobind Singh seeking to make his peace with him. The Guru accepted the offer and agreed to keep at Anandpur a representative of the Raja. The envoy who came, acted more as a spy than as an ambassador of goodwill, yet the Guru treated him with kindness. Following Ajmer Chand's example, other hill rulers also made conciliatory approaches. At Rawalsar, near Mandi, where the Guru had gone with his family for the annual fair, several of the rajas met him personally. They were all charmed by his courtesy and goodwill and entreated him to forget and forgive their former transgressions. The Guru had no malice towards anyone and believed what they said. He invited them to his camp and gave them a cordial reception.

But true to his character, Ajmer Chand was tempted by the first opportunity that offered of assailing the Guru. Two Mughal generals, Said Beg and Alif Khan, were passing by on their way from Lahore to Delhi, each with five thousand men. Ajmer Chand persuaded them to assault the Guru promising them to pay Rs.1,000 daily for their assistance. The generals detoured towards Anandpur, but before they had reached there, Said Beg, hearing stories of Guru Gobind Singh's holiness, detached himself from the invading army. He returned to fight on the Guru's side when the battle was at a critical stage. This dispirited Alif Khan who retired from the contest along with his men. Said Beg remained with the Guru to spend the rest of his days in his company. He broke away from the Emperor, gave his wealth to the Sikhs and continued to be their ally in their struggles against the Mughals.

Anandpur faced another attack on 2 December 1703. Ajmer Chand came with 10,000 men picked from the armies of several of the hill chieftains. There were not more than 800 Sikh to defend the town. They saw their best chance in coming out and making a sudden charge. This onslaught had the effect of creating confusion in the ranks of the opponents. Ajmer Chand was the first to flee the field. Other rajas made a bid to check the rout and stood firmly behind their men. The battle raged furiously for some time, but the hillmen were eventually forced to withdraw. Alam Singh and Ude Singh added further lustre to their names as warriors by their deeds of chivalry. "The divine man won the victory and the rajas made their surrender," sang poet Saina Pat.

Anandpur was so much the focus of attention that still another host came to reduce it to submission. This was the Mughal force despatched under imperial orders, with Said Khan as the commander. Most of the Sikhs had gone to their homes to meet their families after long periods of absence, and there were only about five hundred men left with the Guru. Yet they jumped into the thick of the battle and fought with their customary tenacity. Two faithful Muslims, Maimun Khan and Said Beg, battled on the Guru's side. The latter was killed when the action was at its fiercest. Riding his famous blue-coloured charger, the Guru made a dash through the ranks and reached where the Mughal commander Said Khan was. He had heard many marvellous stories about the Guru from his sister who was the wife of Pir Buddhu Shah, and instantly recognized him. All intent of war vanished from his heart and, dismounting his horse, he touched the Guru's stirrup to pay him homage. He could fight the Guru no longer and withdrew from the contest. This was the end of his career as a soldier, and he spent the rest of his life in prayer.

A Brahman of Bassi, near Hoshiarpur, came to Anandpur bewailing that his bride had been forcibly abducted and petitioned the Guru in pathetic tones to have his bride restored to him. The Guru sent his son, Ajit Singh, with 100 horses, to rescue the woman. Ajit Singh displayed remarkable promptitude and initiative in carrying out the task. Marching with speed, he surprised the Pathans in their village and recovered the woman from their captivity. She was restored to her husband who was full of gratitude and praise for young Ajit Singh.

Anandpur had been subject to constant raid and encroachment since 1700. In the winter of 1704, a much more formidable force was assembled by the Mughal officers and hill rajas than had ever taken the field against the Sikhs, and their religious capital faced the worst challenge in its short, but eventful, history. Ajmer Chand journeyed to the Deccan to apply in person to Aurangzeb for assistance against Guru Gobind Singh. The Emperor had heard with anxiety reports of the growth of the Sikh faith and the influence its preceptor commanded. He was in a fury to see the alarming petition now laid before him and immediately issued orders to the governors of Sirhind and Lahore to lead an expedition against the Sikhs and capture their Guru.

Anandpur was celebrating with usual Sikh ceremony the festival of Diwali for which a large number of Guru Gobind Singh's followers had come from outside. When the news arrived of a mighty host marching upon them, their spirits rose and the prospect of striving for the Guru's cause, and, if fortune favoured, of winning the crown of martyrdom pleased their hearts. Many of them decided not to return home and stayed on in anticipation of the approaching contest. The hill rajas, who had long been contriving a combined campaign on this large scale, gleefully joined the Mughal force along with their troops. The Subadar of Lahore met them at Ropar. The allied army came, under the command of Wazir Khan of Sirhind, eager for war and revenge. Their battle-cries resounded like thunder through the valley, striking terror even into the stony hills around.

The Sikhs furnished themselves with weapons of war so that none remained unarmed. The supplies were laid in and the Guru addressed his followers in inspiring words and repeated the following quatrain of his own composition:

Blest in this world is the life of him who repeateth God's name and keepeth himself in readiness for contest.

This body is impermanent and shall not abide forever...

Make it a house of resignation;
Light thine understanding as a lamp;
Take the broom of divine knowledge into thy hand.
And sweep away the filth of timidity.

So great was the enthusiasm among the Sikhs, that several of them donned saffron clothes in token of their resolve to fight the opponents to the death. They said, "Men have but four days to live in this world. Why should we not endeavour to obtain the exalted dignity of martyrdom while we may?"

The Sikhs met the advancing army with fire from their guns which had a devastating effect. This was supplemented by a quick charge of horsemen, supported by musket-fire by the infantry from behind the ramparts. This kind of planned and aggressive action was totally unexpected by the invaders. Being in the valley below, they had no protection against the fire and, consequently, suffered heavy losses. Two Sikhs, Ude Singh and Daya Singh, charged into the opponents' ranks, with their men committing further damage.

The commanders of the allied troops were surprised by the swiftness of these tactics. They thought the only way they could retrieve the situation was by storming the fortress where the Sikhs had taken up positions. This they attempted with all their force. The tempo of the battle became fiercer and, for the space of three hours, horse and foot were locked in frenzied combat without relenting pace. When the armies disengaged themselves at sundown, the allied forces counted 900 of their soldiers as killed. The Mughal generals could not believe that what the hill rajas had described as a "low rabble" was capable of such brave and orderly action.

The battle on the second day was equally severe. Casualties on both sides were heavy, yet the issue remained inconclusive. The Sikhs repulsed stoutly every assault that was made to capture the fort. Guru Gobind Singh himself took part in the operations mounted on his favourite steed. So did his son, Ajit Singh, who won the admiration of foe and friend alike by his deeds of valour.

At the end of the day's fighting, some of the Guru's followers complained to him that a Sikh, called Kanhaiya, had been giving water and succour not only to the wounded Sikhs but to the enemy also. The Guru asked Kanhaiya if that was true. "Yes, my Lord, it is true in a sense," spoke Kanhaiya. "I have been giving water to everyone who needed it on the field of battle. But I saw no Mughals or Sikhs there. I saw only the Guru's face in everyone." The Guru, pleased with the reply, blessed him and told his Sikhs that Kanhaiya had understood his teaching correctly.

Despaired of reducing the city by direct assault, the invading army planned to lay siege to it with a view to cutting off all supplies and eventually forcing the garrison to submission. The scheme was executed with thoroughness and the place was closely invested barring all entry as well as exit. The Sikhs were watchful and wary and utilized this interval to strengthen their fortifications. The troops were split into five divisions. One contingent of five hundred was placed under the command of Ajit Singh, and stationed in the fort of Kesgarh. Another contingent of the same strength, under Sher Singh and Nahar Singh, was charged with the defence of Lohgarh. The third division, under Alam Singh and Ude Singh, was to look after Agampura and the surrounding parts of the town. Mohkam Singh, one of the Five Beloved, took charge of Holgarh, while Guru Gobind Singh, with the rest of the Sikhs, positioned himself in Anandgarh. The population was instructed to stay behind the fortifications and beware of any sudden attack.

The Mughal commander pushed the siege further and it ultimately began to tell on the beleaguered garrison. The provisions inside ran short and the grain sold at a rupee a seer and was yet not easily available at that price. The Sikhs searched for it by making assaults on the enemy camps, but this grew increasingly difficult as the vigilance became stricter. Every nightly expedition for food now proved costlier in human life. For water Anandpur depended on a hill stream which was diverted by Ajmer Chand's men. This made the situation still more precarious. "Four Sikhs," as the poet describes, "used to go out to fetch water. While two of them attempted to bring water, the other two engaged in deadly battle to make this possible."

As the siege became protracted, the hardship of the garrison increased. Yet their spirit remained undaunted, and they did not relax in the defence of the town. But with every day that passed the position worsened until some of the Sikhs approached Guru Gobind Singh and suggested evacuation. He was not in favour of this, and rejected the idea. A few Sikhs wavered in their resolution and insisted on leaving. The Guru told them that they could go, if they were prepared to disown him. Some of them actually wrote a statement disowning him and left.

Meanwhile, message came from the Mughal generals and the rajas as also from the Emperor that, if the Guru evacuated Anandpur, the siege would be lifted and the armies would withdraw. They vowed by their religious books that they would not harm him or his Sikhs when leaving the city. The Guru knew that they did not mean what they had communicated to him. But any effective defence of Anandpur was now impossible owing to the lack of foodstuffs and other supplies. The privations of the Sikhs had become too acute for the Guru to disregard. So he decided to evacuate the fort. On the night of 5-6 December 1705, he left Anandpur. He was preceded by a party consisting of his mother, his two younger sons, and such of the men as were unfit for action. Before mounting his horse, he visited his father's shrine to recite prayer. He entrusted the place to a Sikh of the Udasi sect, called Gurbakhsh, and rode out, with Daya Singh, Alam Singh and Ude Singh in front of him, the second batch of baptized Sikhs on his left, Mohkam Singh on his right, his two elder sons and Himmat Singh behind him, with about five hundred Sikhs in the rear.

CHAPTER - 10

Martyrdoms of Sahibzadas

Guru Gobind Singh cast one last look over the tall ramparts on the hills of Anandpur turning into shadows in the darkness of night, and set his course towards the plains of Punjab. Departing from Anandpur, where he had lived for thirty years of his life, could not have been without a pang. There, he had spent the happiest period of his boyhood under the loving care of his father, Guru Tegh Bahadur, and grown to his responsibilities as the inheritor of the legacy of Guru Nanak and as the spiritual leader of a community intensely devoted to his person. There, he had written poetry and sat for long hours in mystical communion, sported with his Sikhs, practised the martial skills and matched his prowess with mighty warriors. There, at Anandpur, his dreams and visions materialized and he touched the springs of an impulse which transformed the people and their destiny. Now, in one of history's strangest turns, he was leaving the place never to see it again in his lifetime. But all this, as he knew, was in fulfilment of some higher purpose.

The party had not yet gone far, when it was set upon by those who had promised it a safe departure. The rearguard, under Ajit Singh, engaged the pursuers. Ude Singh, a warrior of excelling valour who had won renown in many a battle, relieved the Guru's young son of the command and held the enemy at bay until he fell in the unequal contest. The Guru had reached the margin of a stream called Sirsa, then in flood with the winter rains. Pressed by the pursuing host, the contingent attempted to go across. This proved a most hazardous enterprise and the horror-filled cold night took its heavy toll. The whole party was scattered. Some of the Sikhs lost their lives in the icy waters of the rivulet. Those who crossed it, dispersed in all directions without knowing where to go. The Guru's mother, *Mata* Gujari, with his two younger sons, Zorawar Singh and Fateh Singh, chanced to meet an old servant of the household, Gangu, who undertook to escort them safely to his village. Similarly, a faithful Sikh resident of Delhi offered to lead the Guru's wives to safety. The Guru's own party was reduced to a bare forty Sikhs and his two elder sons, Ajit Singh and Jujhar Singh.

The troops, hotly in pursuit of him, were joined by fresh reinforcements coming from Delhi and by local Ranghars and Gujjars who were willing to take any opportunity to attack him. The Guru took shelter in a mud-walled house belonging to a Sikh of his in the village of Chamkaur. He arranged for the defence of this improvised fortress by splitting his small force into groups to look after the four sides of it. Alam Singh and Man Singh were appointed sentinels, whereas he himself, with his two sons and Daya Singh and Sant Singh, took up position on the top storey.

The massive army came surging forward like dark clouds and threw a tight ring round the village. The poet compared the Guru thus encompassed to the moon surrounded by the stars on all sides. With the approach of the pursuers began the epic struggle for forty odd men against a multitudinous horde – a saga of purest heroism and sacrifice. In batches, each of five, the Sikhs went forth to contend with the army outside and meet certain death. None of them winced or turned his back towards the enemy. In fact, they vied with one another in obtaining priority to go out into the field of battle. Most moving were the moments when the Guru's sons, Ajit Singh and Jujhar Singh, aged eighteen and fourteen, respectively, begged their father one after the other to be allowed to court death in the only befitting manner open to the Guru's Sikhs. The Guru cheerfully conceded their requests and, seeing them fall in battle rendered his gratitude to Akal Purakh for having been able to restore to Him faithfully what He had been pleased to grant him.

In the chivalrous band led by Ajit Singh was Alam Singh, hero of many such contests. Among others who fell martyrs at Chamkaur were Mohkam Singh, Sahib Singh and Himmat Singh, three of the *Panj Piare* and the second batch of Sikhs baptized by the Guru at the time of inauguration of the Khalsa. Each of the Sikhs fought with daring stubbornness and gave his life dearly. One prevailed against many. The Guru's sons displayed extraordinary courage and fought like veterans. They caused much destruction in the opponents' ranks before they were overcome. Ajit Singh, as the poet said, impaled many Pathans with his spear and, when the spear broke, he piled the sword with equally fatal effect. Jujhar Singh tore his way through the Mughal army like a crocodile bursting through the waters of a stream.

Exasperated by the havoc made by the impertinently small batches of Sikhs, the Subadar of Lahore attempted to take the place by storm, but had to retreat under raining arrows from the besieged. Nahar Khan, an officer of the imperial army, tried to scale the wall of the house, but was shot down. By nightfall the Guru was left with five Sikhs – the only survivors of his brave and numerous warriors. Seeing how hopeless the situation was, the Sikhs made a resolution and entreated their Master to leave Chamkaur. They said that, if the Guru lived, the Khalsa would flourish again. The Guru did not wish to abandon the position, whatever the odds, but had to bow to what amounted to the command of the Five.

Two of the Sikhs, Sant Singh and Sangat Singh, offered to remain in the fortress and the other three, Daya Singh, Dharam Singh and Man Singh, prepared to accompany the Guru. As he emerged from the portals of the fortress, he extinguished, with a shower of arrows, the night-torches of the besieging troops. This created chaos among them and the Guru escaped unmolested. In the morning, the battle was resumed and the two Sikhs holding the "fort" rained arrows on the army which encircled them. But the Mughal soldiers soon scaled the walls and thought they were going to capture the Guru. Sant Singh who, they were sure, was Guru Gobind Singh and his companion were decapitated. Their heads were to be presented to the Emperor, but the commander of the Mughal army was sorely disappointed when he learnt that neither of the Sikhs was Guru Gobind Singh.

The battle of Chamkaur took place on 7 December 1705. Writing about it subsequently in his letter, in Persian, addressed to Aurangzeb, Guru Gobind Singh said, "What could forty famished men do when such a large number fell on them unawares. The oath-breakers attacked them abruptly with swords, arrows and muskets. I was forced to engage in the combat, and I fought to the best of my ability. When an affair passes beyond all remedy, it is but righteous to have recourse to the sword...Clad in black, your army came like thick swarms of bees and made a sudden charge. Every soldier of yours, who advanced beyond his defences to attack my position, fell deluged in blood. Such of your soldiers as committed no aggression received no injuries at our hands...The Khawaja remained behind cover and did not come forth like a man. Had I but seen his face, I would certainly have bestowed an arrow on him, too. Many were killed on both sides by arrows, bullets and the earth turned red like a tulip. Heads and legs lay in heaps as if the field was littered with balls and sticks. The arrows whizzed, the bows twanged and the great tumult reached the skies. The whizzing of arrows put terror into the hearts of the mightiest of warriors. But how could forty, even of the bravest, succeed when opposed by a countless host?"

In the battle of Chamkaur were killed two of Guru Gobind Singh's four sons. On a single day the two tender and promising youths, in their teens yet, stepped out, one after the other, into the gory field and, within a few hours of each other, fell fighting valiantly before the eyes of their father, delighting his heart with their daring and skill. Not far from there, at Sirhind, within less than a week of this blood-stained morning, his two remaining sons, not yet in their teens, faced the executioner's sword with equal courage. The story of the unique sacrifice and testimony to truth rendered by the two innocent children, aged nine and seven, respectively, is as poignant as it is morally elevating.

Gangu, who had taken charge of the younger sons of the Guru and their grandmother after the calamitous Sirsa crossing, betrayed his trust. His guileless wards unquestioningly followed him to his village, Saheri, and were more than contented with whatever refreshment and hospitality his home provided. At night, *Mata* Gujari slept on a mattress spread out on the floor of the attic, hugging closely to her heart the little children weary from her gruesome journey. Gangu stole from her scanty belongings her saddle-bag containing money and, when she discovered the loss upon waking next morning, he feigned ignorance and protested vehemently, saying that this was a strange reward he was receiving for helping the members of a rebel's family and giving them asylum.

Making loud protestations in this manner, he walked out and went to the village headman and informed him of the presence of Guru Gobind Singh's mother and children in his house. Together they proceeded to meet the next higher official, the Ranghar chief of Morinda, in hope of a handsome recompense for delivering to the authorities such a valuable piece of intelligence. The chief was very happy to have important hostages so easily within his reach. He set out at once with a batch of soldiers for the village of Saheri, and took the Guru's children and his mother into custody.

The prisoners were handed over to Nawab Wazir Khan of Sirhind who had led out expeditions against the Guru. He ordered them to be confined in a tower of the fort at Sirhind. The following day, 9 December 1705, the Guru's sons were summoned to appear before him. The Ranghar went to bring them from the tower. For the grandmother this was a most painful ordeal. She could not bear to let her grandsons be out of her sight for a single moment; trusting them now to the tender mercies of those intent on bringing about the destruction of their father and what was heart wrenching to their grandmother. She was not at all willing to part with her precious treasure until

Zorawar Singh, the elder of her grandsons, spoke and urged her to let them go. "They will not let us escape. We must go and face the Suba," he said. The grandmother kissed them both, crossed her frail hand over their heads and muttered many blessings for them as the two brothers turned round to accompany the Ranghar.

Reaching the court of the Subadar, they uttered with one voice the Sikh greeting: Wahiguru *ji ka Khalsa, Wahiguru ji ki Fateh.* This boldly uttered cry and their confident demeanour astonished everyone present in the court. One of the ministers, Sucha Nand by name, broke the silence and told the young boys that their father, two elder brothers and all their companions had been killed at Chamkaur and that their only hope of escaping the fated end was in bowing before the Nawab and accepting Islam.

Zorawar Singh spoke in a determined tone: "We have been taught to bow before God and the Guru only, and before none else. As for accepting Islam, we have in our veins the blood of Guru Hargobind, Guru Tegh Bahadur and Guru Gobind Singh. None can force us to abjure the faith of our forefathers."

Everyone was amazed to hear this bold reply, especially Wazir Khan, who had thought that the conversion of such brave children would be a gain to Islam. He addressed them directly and said that he would spare their lives, give them estates and marry them to the daughters of nobles highly renowned in the realm, if they renounced their faith. Zorawar Singh looked at his younger brother and, reinforced by the assurance and steadfastness in his eyes, said, "We seek neither estate, nor position. We shall forfeit our lives, but not our faith. Nothing you can offer us will ever tempt us. This worldly authority is not everlasting. The cruelties of the Turks will prove their own ruin."

Wazir Khan ordered the children to be taken to the prison cell and brought before him the following morning. Men were put to cajole and frighten them into submission. But they remained determined and the next day they behaved in the court with the same dignity and firmness of manner as they had shown at the time of their first appearance. The Nawab was now mad with rage and wished to give them the severest punishment. Nawab Sher Muhammad Khan of Malerkotla, who happened to be present, earnestly pleaded that the children were too young and innocent to be punished under the law. He urged that they should not be held responsible for what their father had done and be allowed to depart. Another courtier contradicted the Nawab of Malerkotla and said that, although the children were young, they were the sons of Guru Gobind Singh and would, in their time, fan the tumults he had started.

On the advice of the Qadi, Wazir Khan ordered Zorawar Singh and Fateh Singh to be bricked up in a wall. When the masonry came chest-high, they were told that they could still save their lives by abjuring their faith. But the children were unyielding as ever. The temporary structure tumbled down, and they were pulled out from underneath the debris unconscious. In this state, they were removed to the prison where they came after some time.

On the morning of 12 December, they were taken to the court for the third time and again given the usual choice. Upon their refusal to be converted, they were slain in the order of their ages by a Ghilzai executioner.

A wealthy Sikh, Todar Mal, hearing of the incarceration of Guru Gobind Singh's children, hastened to Sirhind to try to secure their release by paying ransom. But he was too late. On learning of what had happened, he proceeded to break the tragic news to *Mata* Gujari. Those three days had been an interminable torment for her. She was consumed with anxiety for the safety of her grandchildren and passed those agonizing days and nights praying for their lives. The news of their execution proved a fatal shock to her in her old age. She fell into a swoon from which she never recovered.

CHAPTER - 11

Chastisement of the Emperor

His two elder sons, along with his Sikhs, having been killed in battle at Chamkaur and he himself having been separated from the three Sikhs with whom he had escaped during the darkness of the night, Guru Gobind Singh reversed a wearisome and lonely way. Besides the sudden reversal in the state of affairs, the Guru's peregrinations from now on had other elements of drama - hair-breadth escapes, *deus ex machina* unexpectedly intervening at the crucial moment and those expected to come to his succour flinching for fear of imperial retribution. One who had kept royal state, had ruled over the hearts of thousands, and commanded armies, was today a barefooted, lorn wayfarer, without food, without shelter and without companion. His feet bleed from blisters caused by his constant roaming through the jungles. There was nothing for him to eat except the leaves of trees. To assuage his acute thirst he had to moisten his lips sometimes with the milk of the bitter wild-growing *akk* (Calotropis-plant). Yet in this condition, he sang gratefully praises of the Lord Almighty. Unshaken was his faith, and undaunted as ever his spirit. Lying on that cold wintry night under the canopy of the open sky in the midst of the desolate jungle of Machhiwara, with his physical frame listless from extreme privation and exhaustion, the Guru spontaneously uttered the following verse:

Soft beds, dear Friend, beloved God, are but a torment
without Thee,
Residence in mansions like living among serpents.
Wine-goblets like the cross; the rim of wineglass like
the dagger.
All this, without Thee, like the keenness of a butcher's
thrust!
To dwell with them in adversity is better, far better
Than revelry in palaces without Thee!

Following the starry chart they had jointly marked out
at the time of leaving Chamkaur, the three Sikhs who had
been diverted from the course and were frantically in
search of the Guru, came upon the spot where he lay resting
his head on a discarded earthen bowl. Overcome by joy
to meet their Guru again, they burst into a loud shout of
greeting, louder beyond the limits of caution in that
fugitive state. An imperial detachment was, in fact,
prowling not far from there. The Sikhs were aware of this,
and they requested the Guru to leave the place forthwith.
During their rambles the previous day, they had seen a
garden with a well of water inside it and escorted their
Master, sleepless and footsore, in that direction. Upon
arriving at the well, the Guru took a bath – his first in several
days. The owner of the garden, Gulaba, was a Sikh by faith
and had visited the Guru at Anandpur. He congratulated
himself on the good fortune which had descended upon
him. He brought a big pot of milk for the Guru and his
Sikhs. After this refreshment, they lay down to have some
sleep, their host and his brother guarding their riskily
earned repose. Later in the day, Gulaba, took them to his
home and put them up in a room on the upper storey he
had lately added to his dwelling.

In spite of the host's best efforts to keep the Guru's presence in his house a secret, people came to know who the visitor was. This made Gulaba fear for his own safety, and he looked for an excuse to suggest to the Guru to depart. At last, he spoke out his fears openly. In the meantime, two Muslims, Ghani Khan and Nabi Khan, learning that the Guru was being pursued by Mughal troops, came to offer him their services. They had visited him at Anandpur and, being in the horse trade, had sold many good animals to him.

Mai Desan, a devotee, who was Gulaba's neighbour, had been spinning cotton for many months, and had a piece of cloth woven from it to present it to the Guru if she might be so fortunate as to see him in her village. She now made the Guru the gift of the length of *Khaddar* she had lovingly preserved for him. On the suggestion of Ghani Khan and Nabi Khan, the cloth was dyed deep blue and robes were made out of it in the style of the apparel of Muhammadan *faqirs*. Wearing those robes, the party left Gulaba's village. The Guru was carried in a palanquin, which Ghani Khan and Nabi Khan lifted in the front and Man Singh and Dharam Singh in the rear, while Daya Singh reverentially swung a *chauri*, or fly-whisk, over him. The occupant of the palanquin was announced as *Uch ka Pir*, which was a *double entendre* signifying a priest of high religious repute, or the priest of *Uch*, a town in south-western Punjab sacred to Muslims.

Near the village of Lall, the party fell in with a contingent of Mughal troops which had been in search of Guru Gobind Singh. Getting suspicious, the commander closely questioned the escort. He, in the end, summoned Qazi Pir Muhammad from the village to clear up the mystery. The Qazi was an old teacher of the Guru and had, at Anandpur, taught him Persian and Arabic. He was a God-fearing Muslim and did not wish Guru Gobind Singh to fall into the hands of those thirsty for his blood. He admonished the soldiers for having obstructed the holy Pir, and asked the officer to let him proceed without any further interference. The commander obeyed, with many apologies to the party.

Travelling in this manner, Guru Gobind Singh reached the village of Hehar. There lived Kirpal Das, the Udasi *mahant*, who had proved his mettle as a warrior in the battle of Bhangani. He made the Guru and his companions welcome. The Guru rewarded the selfless and arduous service rendered by Ghani Khan and Nabi Khan with presents of gold bracelets and a *hukamnamah*, commending them to the faithful as worthy of esteem and attention. This document is still in the possession of their descendants, and the Sikhs avidly seek to see it and to express their obligation for the debt they owe to the family. Sadly and reluctantly, Ghani Khan and Nabi Khan took their leave of the Guru.

Life of ease as the head of a hermitary had quenched the old fire in Kirpal Das. The thought of the authorities discovering that he was harbouring an outlaw made him panicky. The Guru, divining the embarrassment his host felt, left Hehar and proceeded to Jatpura where Rai Kalha, the Muslim chief of Rai Kot, received him with much genuine warmth and courtesy. He considered it his good fortune to have had this opportunity of entertaining Guru Gobind Singh. He sent one of his servants, Mahi, to Sirhind to bring news of the Guru's mother and sons, who were rumoured to have been taken captives by the Nawab. What

Mahi learnt at Sirhind, he could not repeat before the Guru or Rai Kalha. The story was too tragic and heart-rending. When urged to relate what he had heard, he sobbed and sadly narrated the sorrowful happenings at Sirhind. Guru Gobind Singh heard the account with perfect composure, but Rai Kalha could not control his emotion and cried bitterly execrating the tyrants. The Guru fell into a prayer of gratefulness for having rendered unto the Almighty what was really His. He asked the Rai to take comfort in Akal's will, and not give way to grief. He appreciated the merciful intervention of the Nawab of Malerkotla and gave him his blessings. The Guru also bestowed his favour on his host, Rai Kalha, and gave him a sword as a present before departing. The sword was considered by the family a security of its prosperity. The Rai honoured it as a keepsake and so did his son. But his grandson carried it with him on a hunting expedition, hurt himself with it while attempting to kill a deer and died of the wound thus sustained. In British days, a descendant of the family presented the sword to the English Deputy Commissioner of Ludhiana who sent it to England.

Guru Gobind Singh's next place of halt was Dina, a village in the former princely state of Nabha. He stayed there long enough to gather once again a band of devoted Sikhs. The nucleus was provided by three brothers – Shamira, Lakhmira and Takht Mall – who lived in the village of Kangar nearby and, despite the Guru's warnings of the risk in associating themselves with him, served him diligently and zealously. They were the grandsons of Jodh Rai, who had helped Guru Hargobind in his battles with the Mughals.

As the news of Guru Gobind Singh's presence in Dina

percolated to Sikhs, they started coming singly and in groups to visit him. Some of them never went back and remained to share with him what adventure the unpredictable future concealed with its womb. The Guru was especially pleased to receive one day Param Singh and Dharam Singh, sons of Bhai Rupa, who had been favoured by Guru Hargobind with the pronouncement that the Sikh faith should ever abide in their family. They brought the Guru an offering of a horse and dress which he accepted with pleasure. He conferred these gifts on Shamira as a token of favour. The descendants of Param Singh and Dharam Singh, known as the Bhais of Bagarian, have continued to be a leading Sikh family through the generations esteemed for its tradition of learning and piety. The Sikh chiefs of Patiala, Faridkot, Nabha, Jind, Kapurthala and Kalsia regard the head of the Bagarian House with special reverence and call upon him to preside over the religious ceremonies in their families.

At Dina, Guru Gobind Singh received a conciliatory letter from Emperor Aurangzeb, inviting the Guru to meet him in the Deccan where he then happened to be. This letter was in response to one addressed to him by the Guru after the battle of Chamkaur. Only a portion of this letter has recently come to light. The second letter, which he wrote from Dina upon receiving the Emperor's communication, is preserved, in the whole, in the *Dasam Granth*. In vigorous Persian verse, it has the same tone and style as its precursor. The Guru called it *Zafarnamah* or the 'Epistle of Victory', and sent Daya Singh and Dharam Singh on the long journey to the south carrying it with them for delivery to the Emperor.

As is evident from the title itself, the letter, more

appropriately a fair-sized poem, in 111 stanzas, was
written in an exalted mood of righteous fervour. It reflects
Guru Gobind Singh's spirit of fearlessness and faith and
high moral ideal. The central theme of the composition
is the presentation of the ethical principle as the supreme
law in matters of public policy as well as in private
behaviour. It condemns what is unjust and cruel and extols
what is true and morally correct. Victory and defeat are
to be judged by the ultimate standards of morality, and
not by temporary material advantage. The epistle was a
severe indictment of Aurangzeb, who was repeatedly
chided for breach of faith in the attack made by the Mughal
troops on the Sikhs after they had vacated Anandpur on
solemn assurances given them by him and his officers.
For the candid and unambiguous terms in which the
Emperor and his policies are castigated in it, the
Zafarnamah should easily be the most forthright essay
in diplomacy known in history. It emphatically reiterates
the sovereignty of morality in the affairs of state as much
as in the conduct of individual human beings and regards
the means as important as the end. Absolute truthfulness
is as much the duty of a sovereign as of any one of the
ordinary citizens.

The letter begins with an invocation to God who is
remembered by Guru Gobind Singh as Eternal, Beneficent,
Bestower of Grace, Remitter of Sins, King of Kings, the
support of the Unhappy, Protector of the Faith, Fountain
of Eloquence, and Author of Revelation. Addressing the
Emperor, he says, "I have no faith in thine oath to which
thou tookest the One God as witness. He who putteth faith
in thine oath is a ruined man... Thou knowest not God and
believest not in Muhammad. He, who hath regard for his

religion, never swerveth from his promise...Were the Prophet himself present here, I would make it my special object to inform him of thy treachery...Everybody ought to be a man of his word, and not utter one thing while he meditateth another." The Guru tells him that, although his four sons had been killed, he remained to continue the strife.

How alien the Emperor was to the spirit of religion is emphasized, not without a touch of sarcasm, in a compliment the Guru pays him. He says, "Fortunate art thou Aurangzeb, king of kings, expert swordsman and rider. Handsome is thy person, and intelligent art thou. Emperor and ruler of the country, thou art clever in administering thy kingdom, and skilled in wielding the sword. Thou art generous to thy co-religionists, and prompt to crush thine enemies. Thou art the great dispenser of kingdoms and wealth. Thy generosity is profuse, and in battle thou art firm as a mountain. Exalted is thy position; thy loftiness is as that of the Pleiades. Thou art the king of kings, and an ornament of the thrones of the world. Thou art monarch of the world, but far from thee is religion."

The moral was that all the qualities enumerated were of no value if one were not humane and truthful in one's dealings with others.

Answering Aurangzeb's invitation for a meeting in the Deccan, the Guru asked him to come and see him at Kangar, close to where he was. He told him that he would not be running any danger on the way, for the entire Brar clan, powerful in that area, was under his (Guru's) command.

CHAPTER - 12

Redemption of the Disunited

Wazir Khan of Sirhind was perturbed to hear of the fresh accretions to Guru Gobind Singh's standard and, on the refusal of Shamira, his host at Dina, to surrender him to his officials, was planning to march an army to capture him. The Guru did not wish the village where he had met with such ready welcome to become the scene of a bloody battle. So he moved on and arrived, by Jalal, at Bhagta. Here he met the descendants of Bhai Bahilo, a much respected Sikh of the time of Guru Arjun, Nanak V. At Kot Kapura, he was received by Kapur Singh, ancestor of the Faridkot family. He took baptism at the hands of Guru Gobind Singh, and entered the brotherhood of the Khalsa. The Guru bestowed on him a sword and a shield which are preserved with reverence by his descendants till today.

News arrived of Wazir Khan's army following steadily behind. Guru Gobind Singh travelled south-east to Dhilwan. His stay at this village was significant for the return, to the fold, of the family of Prithi Chand, the eldest brother of Guru Arjun, who had broken away to set up a rival sect. Baba Kaul, his descendant who lived at Dhilwan, came to meet the Guru and presented him with a dress which he put on, discarding the blue robes he had been wearing. Of these old garments, a small piece was preserved by him from which originated the blue dress of the Akalis, or Nihangs.

Baba Kaul's grandson received the Sikh baptism rescinding the family's enmity with the House of Guru Nanak.

The Guru did not remain in Dhilwan long and proceeded towards Kotha Prithi Chand, later known as Kotha Guru, and set up camp in a jungle near the village. During his sojourn in the south-east Punjab, communication was re-established with Sikhs fallen apart from the central rallying point which Anandpur had been for the entire body of the faithful until its isolation by the besieging Mughal armies. Many new converts were made and, once again, a band of devoted Sikhs ready to dare and die for their Master gathered round him. The Sikh commonwealth was put in the process of recovery of its cohesion and dynamism and its functional framework.

Clash with Wazir Khan's forces now seemed imminent and the Guru wished to take the field at a place where water would be easily accessible. Khidrana was one such spot in those sandy deserts suggested to the Guru, and he set out immediately along with his Sikhs. In the village of Jaitu, he was again visited by the Brar chief, Kapur Singh, who gave him one Khana as an escort to guide his way to Khidrana.

The Sikhs who had deserted the Guru at Anandpur were soon remorseful of their action. Their feeling of repentance was sharpened when, upon reaching their villages, they were upbraided by their families for having forsaken the Guru in the hour of difficulty. Even their womenfolk chafed them for their cowardliness and offered to exchange their skirts for their men's dress and go out to battle for the Guru. Further news of the Guru and his family caused much concern among the Sikhs and their sympathizers. The Sikhs of Majha met in an assembly at Patti, near Amritsar, to devise means of making reparation for the faithlessness of those who had renounced their allegiance to him and had returned home from Anandpur. In the midst of much spirited talk was heard the counsel of despair, however faint, repeating the familiar argument about the futility of fighting against authority. In conclusion, it was decided to send some of their representatives to meet the Guru. A body of Sikhs, consequently, left for the Malwa to seek him out, some determined to indemnify with their blood their past apostasy in disowning him and others hopeful of dissuading him from the conflict with the rulers. Many more Sikhs joined the party on the way and, by the time it met the Guru in the neighbourhood of Khidrana, it had swelled to a fairly large contingent.

It was most tender scene as the Sikhs greeted him with half-choked cries of *Wahiguru ji ka Khalsa, Wahiguru ji ki Fateh*. Every heart was overcome by emotion and every eye was full of tears, some of penitence and others of joy, at seeing the Guru who had come through such troublous times. The Guru treated them with affection as they came forward one by one to pay homage to him. The Mughal expedition was hotly in pursuit and there was no time to lose. Yet a few of the party which had just arrived said that the Guru had already lost much and they could hope to gain nothing from continuing the struggle except further suffering. They offered to bring about reconciliation between the Guru and the Mughal Emperor. The naive proposal amused the Guru. He said that, if compromise had been made with intolerance and tyranny, Guru Arjun need not have suffered the torture, nor should Guru Tegh Bahadur have been beheaded. He invited such of the Sikhs as were ready to join him in resisting the attacking host in vindication of the principles of justice and freedom to come with him. Saying these words, the Guru proceeded towards Khidrana. Most of the Sikhs present followed by, while some paused finally to return to their homes.

The Khidrana pond was the only reservoir of water for miles in that vast desert and the Sikhs wished to occupy it before engaging the Mughal army. Guru Gobind Singh, along with the advance party he was leading, posted himself on a sand hillock, nearly a mile away. The Sikhs following him halted at the lake and, to draw off the pursuing force from the Guru's trail, they unfolded their sheets and coverlets and spread them out on the surrounding trees. This stratagem turned the place into what looked like the tents of an army. A shrine called Gurdwara Tambu Sahib, or the place of holy tents, stands on that spot now.

Wazir Khan's men turned in the direction of the "tents". Their spirits waxed to see such a small force in front of them. The belief that Guru Gobind Singh was among the Sikhs on the opposite side, brought to bay in the long run, touched their ardour with deadly resolve, and they made a spirited charge shouting their religious war-cries. The Sikhs stood firm and fought back. Those of them, who sought to be re-admitted to the Guru's favour by winning absolution for their previous act of unfaithfulness, had but one wish and that was to die heroically for him. In the face of the resolute resistance offered by the Sikhs, the Mughal troops felt helpless. They were further confounded by a steady shower of arrows that Guru Gobind Singh and his Sikhs maintained from their vantage-point. Wazir Khan reproached them with cowardice as he found them unsteady in their ranks. He reminded them of their superior numbers and of the insignificance of the adversary and roused them, in the name of holy war, to a renewal of the offensive. There followed a reckless burst of action, in which both sides displayed extraordinary steadfastness.

They suffered severe losses and fought themselves to exhaustion. Parched with thirst and assailed from the rear by Guru Gobind Singh and his followers, the Mughal troops were at last forced to retire. This was on 29 December 1705.

When, at the end of the fighting, Guru Gobind Singh came to the scene of action, he found his Sikhs killed almost to a man. He went about wiping their bloodstained faces and praising and blessing each one of them for his endurance and loyalty. A Sikh, Mahan Singh, lay at the last gasp, eager for a sight of the Guru before he died. When the Guru came to him, he folded his enfeebled hands to greet him. A flicker of light shone in his eyes at his wish having been fulfilled at last. The Guru put his hand affectionately on his forehead, and promised him any boon he might ask of him. Mohan Singh said, "I have seen the Guru's face and have nothing more left to desire." When the Guru insisted on his making a request, he submitted that he coveted neither any worldly advantage nor deliverance. But, if the Guru had forgiven them, he would entreat him to cancel the deed of renunciation he and some of his companions had signed before deserting him at Anandpur. The paper, which the Guru had carried with him through all these difficult months, was torn. This gave Mahan Singh the satisfaction he had longed for, and he died in peace. The Guru counted lying on the battlefield the forty Sikhs who had disclaimed him at Anandpur and had now earned remission for their error with their martyr's blood. The forty dead were blessed by the Guru as the Forty Immortals or Saved Ones (*muktas*). Their deeds of heroism have become part of the Sikhs' daily prayer, and are recounted by hundreds of thousands of the faithful at least twice every day. Khidrana came to be known after them as Muktsar, the Pool of Liberation. Every year a big assembly is held at this place to celebrate the redemption of the disunited. Pilgrims come from all over the country and renew their faith by recalling those brave events.

The sole survivor of the Khidrana Sikhs was Mai Bhago, the woman-warrior, who had led the fugitives back to the Guru's presence with a view to securing them his pardon and had fought in the battle bravely spitting several of the hostile soldiers with a spear. She lay wounded on the battlefield and felt exceedingly happy to see the Guru and to learn that the abjurers had been reunited and her purpose so successfully accomplished.

There were many withered *mal*-trees on the plain where the battle had been fought. The Guru ordered those to be cut and collected to form a large funeral pyre for the Sikhs who had been killed. Setting fire to the pile with his own hands, he sat down under a tree and said, "These men are saved and have attained the dignity of holy devotees and saints." The *Kirtan Sohila* was then read and *karahprasad* distributed.

CHAPTER - 13

Repose at Damdama

Guru Gobind Singh left Khidrana to continue his tour of the Malwa territory and spread the gospel of Guru Nanak. This tract, inhabited by sturdy and straightforward Jat clans, had already been influenced by Sikh teaching, especially during the visits of Guru Hargobind, Guru Har Rai and Guru Tegh Bahadur. The simple, practical and liberating tenets of the new faith appealed to these freedom-loving people, alien to metaphysical niceties and sophisticated rituals. The geography of the area in which they lived gave them immunity from frequent interference by the Mughal governors in Punjab. So they received the Guru as well as his precept with open arms. They entertained him and his party of Sikhs without any fear of the ruling authority and felt privileged to be instructed by him.

Passing through several villages and healing many a parched soil, Guru Gobind Singh arrived in Lakkhi Jungle, a forest between the towns of Bhatinda and Kot Kapura. He was impressed by the seclusion and freedom it afforded and decided to stop there awhile. Soon the forest became alive with the holy chants and with the tramp of the pilgrims' caravans. Large numbers of them came to see the Guru after a long separation – a period marked by harsh, cataclysmal events. But there was no trace on his face of the bitter and violent days.

Guru Gobind Singh's abode in Lakkhi Jungle became an oasis in the midst of that sandy desert. Inspiration sprang forth from here, as had happened at Anandpur, for a more vigorous and meaningful living. People came in ever-increasing numbers to partake of this message. The Guru sealed them for his own by investing them with baptism and the insignia. Sikhism thus took firm root in this region. The converts to the Khalsa baptism and their descendants proved to be the bedrock of the new faith in this part of the country and played a significant role in its history, both in tearing down the fell hand of tyranny and in raising the religious commonwealth to sovereignty in Punjab. Here in Lakkhi Jungle, a Muslim faqir, Ibrahim, received the baptism and took the vows of his new faith. He was renamed Ajmer Singh. His wish was never to abandon the presence of the Guru. He became one of his closest associates and accompanied him when he departed from Lakkhi Jungle to resume his travels.

The Guru proceeded on his journey and, meeting his Sikhs in several of the villages on the way, reached the vicinity of Talwandi Sabo (20 January 1706). He ordered the top of a sand hill to be levelled, took off his armour and sat down on the flattened platform to rest. The spot was known thereafter as Damdama Sahib, i.e. the place of repose, and the Guru remained there for nine months. For the first time, since leaving Anandpur, he was able to stay in one locality undisturbed for any considerable period.

Bhai Dalla, the village landlord, who was one of the Guru's followers, presented himself and pressed him to put up in his fort. But he refused, saying that he preferred to stay outside. Entertainment was accepted at Dalla's house, but only for five days after which the Guru's kitchen opened. Yet Dalla wished to serve the Guru in whatever way he could and took every available opportunity to fulfil his heart's desire by attending to any of the wants of the Guru or those of his Sikhs.

One day he expressed his regret to the Guru that he was not able to render him any service in the troubled days when he underwent such great suffering. If he had but known, he would have sent for his assistance, his men who were so well trained and experienced. Dalla had not yet quite finished speaking about the soldierly qualities of his men, when a party of Sikhs arrived from Lahore with a musket as a present for the Guru. The Guru admired the weapon and said that it must be tested straightway. He asked Dalla if he would be so good as to send for two cf his soldiers to serve as targets for testing the range of the musket. Dalla thought this to be a strange demand, and felt that he would not be able to persuade any of his men to offer himself for sacrifice in this way. Meanwhile, the Guru saw two of his Sikhs, father and son, of a so-called low caste, tying their turbans, and beckoned them to come. Both came running, wrapping hurriedly around their heads the turbans as they tried to outdo each other in the race. They stood facing the musket, one craning his neck above that of the other in order to be the first one to receive the bullet. Dalla was repentant for having spoken vainly of his soldiers, as the moral the Guru aimed at became evident to him. The Guru told him that his object was not to disparage him or his men. Such of the Sikhs as received the sacrament of steel, the *amrit*, stirred with the sword's edge, shed, said the Guru, all fear of death and dedicated themselves to the Khalsa Panth. This was the secret of their fearlessness and loyalty to him.

Dalla himself joined the fold by taking the baptism and received the name of Dall Singh.

Dall Singh had a message from Nawab Wazir Khan, asking him under pain to severe displeasure and punishment to surrender his guest. He declined to oblige him and wrote to him that he should never expect him to commit such a sin. His one wish was ever to abide in the company of the Guru. He further told Wazir Khan that, if he tried to take them by force, they would retire to the recesses of the forest where his men, in case they pursued them, should come to harm as they did at Khidrana.

The Guru acknowledged Dall Singh's devotion, but did not want to endanger his position. He expressed the wish to see the old fort of Bhatinda, not far from there, and be thus away from Talwandi Sabo for some time. Arriving at Bhatinda, the Guru stayed in a room on the top of the fort, driving away from there a tyrant who had held the town and the surrounding area in terror. A Gurdwara, built by Maharaja Amar Singh of Patiala, commemorates the Guru's visit.

Making brief halts in some of the villages on the way, the Guru returned to Damdama Sahib. *Mata* Sundari and *Mata* Sahib Devan arrived from Delhi to join him. They burst into tears recalling the cruel and sorrowful deaths of the four young sons. The Guru tried to console them and said that they had died worthily and attained eternal life. Their brave deeds would be remembered and inspire emulation. "What does it matter if the four died? They died that these thousands might live," said the Guru, pointing towards the Sikhs congregated around him.

Damdama became the point of reunion. Many old Sikhs came here in search of the Guru and felt immensely rewarded by a sight of him. The spirit of hilly Anandpur was revived in sandy Damdama. Early morning choruses of holy harmony, stirring enunciations of the doctrine by the Guru and devotional and martial balladry – everything designed to reshape and re-illumine men's souls – were the order of the day once again.

Bhai Mani Singh, who enjoyed wide repute for his learning, was among those who rejoined him at Damdama Sahib. The Guru proposed to prepare an authorized version of the Adi Granth which, since its compilation by Guru Arjun, had several discrepant transcriptions. This was considered to be a most sacred task and a separate tent was put up in which the Guru and Bhai Mani Singh daily worked long hours without interruption. The first copy of the Adi Granth had been transcribed by Bhai Gurdas at Guru Arjun's dictation. Now it was the privilege of Bhai Mani Singh who wrote as Guru Gobind Singh spoke. The original contained the hymns of the first five Gurus and of certain *sufis* and *bhaktas*, such as Farid, Kabir, Ravi Das. Guru Gobind Singh added to the text the compositions of his father, Guru Tegh Bahadur, but none of his own. His writings were subsequently collected by Bhai Mani Singh and compiled into what came to be known as the *Dasam Granth*, the Book of the Tenth Master.

The finalization of the Adi Granth at Damdama Sahib was celebrated with appropriate ceremony and thanksgiving. The Guru cast the ink and the reeds used in transcribing the volume into the pool close to the tent under which the work had been completed, and said that Damdama would be the Kashi or Banaras of the Sikhs and become famous as a seat of learning. "Many," he foretold, "will study here and become learned. They will cast off their ignorance, and rise into authors, sages, poets and commentators." The tank has since been known as Likhan Sar, the pool of literary inspiration. The place, also called Guru-ki-Kashi, has always represented a vital and distinguishable tradition of Sikh scholarship and Damdama school- men and interpreters of the sacred texts have ranked among the most influential and authoritative. Until the time the Holy Book began to be printed, copies transcribed at Damdama Sahib were especially prized. Gurmukhi calligraphy of the place was accepted as standard and formed the basis of characters later moulded for printing.

At Damdama Sahib, Bhais Taloka and Rama, ancestors of the Phulkian chiefs, were baptized by Guru Gobind Singh himself. Their ancestor, Phul, had been favoured by Guru Har Rai with the promise of sovereignty coming into his family. They had themselves rendered unique service to the House of the Guru by performing, in face of mortal peril, the obsequies of the Guru's two sons fallen in the battle of Chamkaur. They received the names of Talok Singh and Ram Singh after baptism. From the former are descended the ruling families of Nabha and Jind, and from the latter that of Patiala. The number of seekers was sometimes so large that *amrit* had to be prepared in big steel vessels. According to tradition, more than a hundred thousand people partook of the elixir and were baptized into the Khalsa fraternity at Damdama Sahib.

The Baisakhi festival, which came off during Guru Gobind Singh's stay there, was kept at Damdama Sahib as the birthday of the Khalsa. Sikhs came from all sides to participate in the festivity and gladden their hearts by a sight of the Guru. The day has since been celebrated at this place annually with great enthusiasm.

CHAPTER - 14

Guruship Passes to the Holy Granth

In spite of its scathing tone, the letter Guru Gobind Singh had sent to Emperor Aurangzeb through Bhai Daya Singh and Bhai Dharam Singh was not taken amiss. The ill and aged Emperor was moved to read it, impressed by the very straight-forwardness and fearlessness of its author who had unshakable faith in God and His justice. He dictated from his sickbed a letter to Mun'im Khan, his Wazir at Delhi, asking him to show friendliness to Guru Gobind Singh, invite him and, then conveying to him the *farman*, send him to the royal presence. The Wazir also was instructed to pay the Guru, out of his confiscated property, as much cash as he desired for his travelling expenses and provide him with a guide. The letter was made over to the Emperor's macebearer, Muhammad Beg, who, along with the Guru's messengers, Daya Singh and Dharam Singh, set out for the north.

Guru Gobind Singh had heard nothing of these developments yet. The only news he had received from Daya Singh, since his departure from Dina with the *Zafarnamah*, was about the difficulty he was encountering in securing a personal audience with the Emperor. He had advised him to wait patiently and written to the Sikhs of Ahmadnagar to help him in the execution of his mission. Having had no further information from Daya Singh and the air becoming thicker day by day with the reports of the failing health of the ninety-year-old Emperor, Guru Gobind Singh decided to go to the Deccan and meet him personally.

The Sikhs at Damdama were dismayed to hear this, most of all Dall Singh who had fondly imagined that the Guru had come to stay in his village permanently and who could not now reconcile himself to separation from him. He and some other prominent Sikhs, such as Dharam Singh, son of Bhai Rupa, Ram Singh and Talok Singh of Phul, Abhai Ram Sodhi of Kotha Guru, Bhai Ram Singh of the Chakk, Bhai Godaria of Bhucho, and Dan Singh Brar importuned the Guru to stay in Damdama. "O King," they said, "you hold court here, and give audience to your friends and disciples. Why then think of a journey to the barren countries of the Deccan?" "I have got work to do there," replied the Guru, "and must go, though there could, undoubtedly, be no spot more fascinating than this Damdama."

Several of the Sikhs mounted their horses to accompany the Guru, but only a few were permitted. Among them were Mani Singh, Param Singh, Dharam Singh, Man Singh, Ram Singh of Bhai Bhagtu's family, and Dan Singh's son, Gurbakhsh Singh Brar. The Guru repeated *ardas* at the shrine of his father, Guru Tegh Bahadur who had himself visited the place during his travels in the tract, and started on the southward journey on 30 October 1706. To spare them the arduousness of a long and difficult journey, *Mata* Sundari and *Mata* Sahib Devan were sent to Delhi under an escort.

The Guru marched by way of Rajputana. He passed through Sirsa, Nauhar (in Bikaner), Madhu Singhana and Pushkar and reached Naraina, also called Dadudwara from the saint Dadu who had lived there. The Guru pitched his tents near the saint's shrine and saluted the tomb by lifting an arrow to his head. The Khalsa took exception to it, and demanded a fine. One of them, Man Singh, quoted the Guru's own verse: *Gor marhi mat bhul na mane*, (worship not even by mistake cemeteries or places of cremation). The Guru immediately offered to pay. The fine was fixed at Rs. 5,000, but a Sikh objected that it was too big a sum and proposed to reduce it to Rs. 500. Another Sikh thought it too little and said the Guru would not feel the loss of such a paltry amount. One of them said that he would not be satisfied with anything under five lakhs, but some of them argued that, though the Guru could even pay that sum, the Khalsa would find it impossible to pay fines in proportion thereafter. They at length asked the Guru to pay Rs. 125 which they spent on the purchase of a kitchen tent.

Guru Gobind Singh was in the neighbourhood of a place, called Kulayat, when Daya Singh, returning from the south, met him. He gave him the details of what had transpired at his interview with the Emperor, and told him that the mace-bearer had gone to Delhi with the royal order issued to Wazir Mun'im Khan. A short time after, news arrived of Aurangzeb's death, on 20th February 1707, at Ahmadnagar. Since the purpose of the Guru's journey was to meet the Emperor, he proceeded no farther, and turned his footsteps northwards. He arrived, along with his *entourage*, at Delhi where *Mata* Sundari and *Mata* Sahib Devan had come direct from Damdama Sahib.

Aurangzeb's death was a signal for the usual war of succession. His three sons – Muazzam, Azam and Kambakhsh – were claimants for the throne. Muazzam, the eldest, who was then on the north-western frontier of the empire without any army or treasure, had himself proclaimed king at Kabul, while Azam assumed the title in the Deccan camp. The object of both of them was the imperial city towards which they made a hurried march. Prince Muazzam was advised by Bhai Nand Lal, a devoted and influential Sikh who had been his trusted *munshi* or secretary, to request Guru Gobind Singh for help. The Guru, who had by now reached near Delhi, had not with him a force large enough to be of any substantial assistance in the contest. Yet the prince wrote to him, seeking his aid and blessings.

Muazzam had the reputation of being a liberal man and, as the eldest son of Aurangzeb, he was the rightful heir to the imperial throne. Unlike his father, he was not bigoted and had given evidence of his broadmindedness and his regard for holy men irrespective of their religious convictions. When sent under imperial orders to punish the hill rajas of Punjab as well as Guru Gobind Singh, he had shown due deference to the spiritual rank of the latter and scrupulously abstained from interfering in his affairs. For these reasons, the Guru considered Muazzam worthy of whatever support he could give him. Never to deny a suppliant was only in keeping with that radiation of the House of Guru Nanak. So he sent some Sikhs under the command of Dharam Singh to defend his right to the crown. The two brothers met each other in battle at Jajau, near Agra, on 8 June 1707. Azam was defeated and killed along with his two adult sons, and Muazzam became Emperor with the title of Bahadur Shah. He conveyed to the Guru the news of his victory and his gratitude through Dharam Singh, leader of the Sikh detachment.

Not long afterwards, Guru Gobind Singh left Delhi for Agra and, visiting Mathura and Brindaban on the way, set up camp in a garden outside the city. On hearing of his arrival, the Emperor extended to him an invitation to meet him which he gladly accepted. He set out under an escort of chosen Sikhs and was received by Bahadur Shah with great honour. The Emperor expressed immense happiness at seeing the Guru and thanked him for his visit and for the help he had given him in the battle of Jajau. Before he departed, Bahadur Shah presented him, in token of his reverence, with a *khil'at*, including a jewelled scarf, a *thukhthukhi* (a bejeweled ornament worn round neck) and an aigrette (*kalghi*). The Guru's attendant who waited outside the hall was called in and he carried the dress of honour to his camp.

This meeting, which took place on 23 July 1707, not only established cordiality of relationship between Guru Gobind Singh and the Emperor, but also became the starting point of parleys between the two on the question of the ruler's attitude towards faiths other than Islam. Both of them agreed to resume these subsequently and the Guru was hopeful that he would be able to return to Punjab at the conclusion of the dialogue that had been opened. He issued letters to his Sikhs to this effect. One of these, addressed to the *sangat* of Dhaul, has been recently traced. Translated into English, it would read:

> To the *sangat* of Dhaul. You are my Khalsa. The Guru will protect you. Repeat Guru, Guru (always remember the Great Master). With all happiness, we came to the *Padshah*. A dress of honour and a jewelled *dhukhdhukhi* worth sixty thousand was presented to us. With the Guru's grace, the other things are also progressing (satisfactorily). In a few days we are also coming. My instruction to the entire Khalsa *sangat*

is to remain united; when we arrive at Kahlur, the entire
Khalsa should come to our presence fully armed. He
who comes shall be happy... Samvat 1764, dated Katik
1st [2, October 1707].

But Bahadur Shah had to leave suddenly for the
Deccan to quell a rebellion by his brother, Kambakhsh.
Guru Gobind Singh, instead of coming to Punjab,
travelled south with him to complete the negotiations.
The two camps marched together and the Guru and the
Emperor took opportunities of making long conversations
on subjects, spiritual and temporal. Sometimes, the Guru
would break away from the caravan to impart his message
to the people of the new territories through which he
was now journeying.

The escorts of the two camps often fell into mutual
wrangling. Some of the Mughal soldiers had fought against
the Sikhs at Anandpur in Wazir Khan's army, and they
inwardly resented the friendly turn in the state's attitude
towards Guru Gobind Singh. They deliberately provoked
the Sikhs who would retaliate. To pacify one such squabble,
the Guru sent Man Singh who was wise and tactful. But
rather than appreciate his peaceful intent, one of the
Mughal escort killed him on the spot. Man Singh had been
a constant companion of the Guru through all
circumstances, and his loss was deeply felt. The Emperor
was sorry to hear of the incident. He ordered the murderer
to be arrested and surrendered to Guru Gobind Singh for
punishment. But the Guru forgave him and let him return
to his camp.

As the Guru passed through the princely cities of
Jaipur and Jodhpur, the Rajput rajas sent their envoys to
wait upon him and do him homage. The camps crossed

the Narbada into the Deccan and travelled farther south to reach Nander, on the Godavari, in August, 1708. The Guru's negotiations with Bahadur Shah remained inconclusive. He found the Emperor evasive, especially when the talk veered round to the tyrannies perpetrated during his father's reign. He also seemed helpless to take any action against fanatical satraps, such as Wazir Khan of Sirhind. The Guru saw little profit in pursuing the parleys any further.

Reaching Nander, Guru Gobind Singh came upon the hermitage of a Bhairagi *sadhu*, Madho Das, who was believed to possess magical powers. Finding him absent from his hut, the Guru laid himself down on his couch to wait for him, while his Sikhs killed a goat to cook meat for the evening meal. Madho Das was furious at this profanation of his monastery, and burned with the desire to chastise the strange visitor for his boldness. But no sooner did he set his eyes on the Guru than all his anger was gone: so was his sorcerous will of which he was greatly proud. He fell at the Guru's feet and called himself his *banda*, or slave. The brief colloquy which took place is set down by Ahmad Shah Batalia in his *Zikr-i-Guruan wa Ibtida-i-Singhan wa Mazhab-i-Eshan*, which was based on contemporary records kept by his ancestors.

Madho Das: Who are you?
Guru Gobind Singh: He whom you know.
Madho Das: What do I know?
Guru Gobind Singh: Think it over in your mind.
Madho Das (after a pause): So you are Guru Gobind Singh.
Guru Gobind Singh: Yes.
Madho Das: What have you come here for?

Guru Gobind Singh: I have come so that I may make you my disciple.

Madho Das: I submit, my Lord, I am a Banda (slave) of yours.

On 3 September 1708, Madho Das was baptized with the rites and vows of the discipline of the Khalsa and given the name of Banda Singh Gurbaksh. The Guru gave him five arrows from his own quiver, and an escort of a few of his chosen Sikhs, and directed him to go to Punjab to carry on the campaign against the cruelty and injustice of the provincial governors. Banda Singh punished Wazir Khan, sacked Sirhind and shook the Mughal rule to its very foundations by his successive victories until he was overcome and seized and cruelly done to death in Delhi in 1716.

Guru Gobind Singh was in environs which wholly pleased his heart. Having lived all his life within hearing of the murmurous music of the flowing waters – at Patna where he was born it was the Ganga; at Anandpur, the Sutlej; at Paonta, the Jamuna – he had a special fascination for a riparian abode. The secluded town of Nander on the margin of the gently moving, slumberous Godavari naturally attracted him and he decided to settle there. But he had not a long earthly span left him.

Nawab Wazir Khan of Sirhind felt apprehensive at the Emperor's conciliatory treatment of Guru Gobind Singh. Their marching together to the South made him extremely jealous, and he charged two of his trusted men with murdering the Guru before his increasing friendship with the Emperor resulted in any harm to himself. These two Pathans pursued the Guru secretly and overtook him at

Nander. They frequently visited the Sikh camp and familiarized themselves with the Guru as well as with his followers. One day as he lay in his chamber resting after the *Rahiras* prayer, one of the Pathans suddenly fell upon him and stabbed him on the left side near the heart. Before he could attack again, Guru Gobind Singh struck him down with his sabre. His companion fell under the swords of the Sikhs who had rushed in on hearing the noise.

When the news reached Bahadur Shah's camp, he sent expert surgeons to attend on Guru Gobind Singh. One of them, it is said, was an Irishman, called Dr.Cole. The injury was healed. But, not long afterwards, as he stretched a powerful bow, the healing wound opened again and bled profusely. This weakened, beyond recovery, the Guru's physical frame which had been through such stormy times.

The Guru called his Sikhs and reminded them how Akal's will had to be cheerfully accepted under all conditions and at all times. He said, "God the Creator and Cherisher of all is alone immortal. Know that the light of the imperishable God whose attributes are permanence, consciousness and happiness, shineth ever in you. Wherefore always abide in cheerfulness, and never give way to mourning. Remember the true Name, Khalsaji. I have attached you to the Immortal God and entrusted you to him. Read the Granth Sahib, or listen to it, so shall your minds receive consolation."

A day before the end came, he asked for the Sacred Volume to be brought forth. To quote Bhatt Vahi Bhadson Parganah Thanesar:

Guru Gobind Singhji mahal dasman beta Guru Tegh Bahadurji ka pota Guru Hargobindji ka parpota Guru Arjunji ka bans Guru Ram Dasji ki Surajbansi gosal gotra Sodhi Khatri basi Anandpur Parganah Kahlur muqam Nander tat Godavari des dakkhan samvat satran sai painsath Katik mas ki chauth shukla pakkhe budhwar ke dihun Bhai Daya Singh se bachan hoya Sri Granth Sahib lai aao. Bachan pai Daya Singh Sri Granth lai aye. Guru ji ne panch paise narial age bheta rakh matha teka. Sarbatt sangat se kaha mera hukam hai meri jagah Sri Granthji ko janana. Jo Sikh janega tis ki ghal thaen paegi Guru tis ki bahuri karega satt kar manana.

Guru Gobind Singh, the Tenth Master, son of Guru Tegh Bahadur, grandson of Guru Hargobind, great-grandson of Guru Arjun, of the family of Guru Ram Das, Surajbansi Gosal clan, Sodhi Khatri, resident of Anandpur, *pargnah* Kahlur, now at Nander, in the Godavari country in the Deccan, asked Bhai Daya Singh, on Wednesday, Katik Chauth, Shukla Pakkh, Samvat 1765 BK/October 6, 1708, to fetch Sri Granth Sahib. In obedience to his orders, Daya Singh brought the Granth Sahib. The Guru placed before it five pice and a coconut and bowed his head before it. He said to the *sangat*, "It is my commandment: Own Sri Granthji in my place. He who so acknowledges it will obtain his reward. The Guru will rescue him. Know this as the truth."

The personal Guruship was thus ended. Succession now passed to the Guru Granth in perpetuity. This was a most significant development in the history of the community. The finality of the Holy Book was a fact rich in religious and social implications. The Book was now the medium of the Divine revelation descended through the Gurus. It was for the Sikhs the perpetual authority, spiritual as well as historical. They lived their religion in response to it. Through it, they were able to observe their faith more fully, more vividly. It was central to all that subsequently happened in Sikh like. From it the community's ideals, institutions and rituals derived their meaning. It constituted the regulative principle for its aspiration and action. It was the integral focus of its psyche.

The Word enshrined in the Holy Book was always revered by the Gurus as well as by their disciples as of divine origin. The Guru was the revealer of the Word. One day the Word was to take the place of the Guru. The line of personal Gurus could not have continued forever. The inevitable came to pass when Guru Gobind Singh declared Guru Granth his successor. It was only through the Word that Guruship could be made everlasting. This, Guru Gobind Singh secured by his uncanny vision and genius. The Guru Granth was henceforth the Guru for the Sikhs - for all time. In their hard, exilic days soon afterwards when they were outlawed and had to seek the safety of the hills and jungles, their most precious possession, which they cherished and which they defended at the cost of their lives, was the Guru Granth.

Guru Gobind Singh uttered a spirited *Wahiguru ji ka Khalsa, Wahiguru ji ki Fateh* to bid his last farewell to the Sikhs - Sikhs who loved him above everything else and had dared and achieved so much under his guidance and inspiration and for whose sake he had considered no endeavour or sacrifice too great. As the Sikhs responded with *Wahiguru ji ka Khalsa, Wahiguru ji ki Fateh,* he left for his heavenly abode in the early hours of 7 October 1708. Thus passed from the earthly scene a great teacher and regenerator of mankind – the anointed messenger who revealed God's ways and will to the people and showed by personal example the ultimate possibilities of the human soul for compassionate as well as for heroic action and for suffering in fulfilment of the highest truth and values known to mankind.

The Sikhs made preparations for his obsequies. The sacred body was placed on the pyre erected inside an enclosure formed of tent-walls and the fire was lit in the midst of chanting of the holy hymns. The *Sohila* was then recited and *karahprasad* was distributed. Away from Punjab and bereft of the physical appearance of the Master, the Sikhs felt an emptiness they had not known before in their history beginning from Guru Nanak. But they remembered the words of the Guru who had blended himself with the Khalsa and exalted them to the pontificate itself. This sense of the indwelling presence of the Guru gradually took hold of them and, in course of time, permeated the collective consciousness of the community. This has been the Sikhs' living belief which shaped the course of their history and led to one of the noblest endeavours in the annals of mankind in the cause of human dignity and freedom.

CHAPTER - 15

Epilogue

66They are remarkably brave, superior in war to all Asiatics. They are remarkable for their simplicity and integrity, so reasonable as never to have recourse to a law-suit, and so honest as neither to require locks to their doors nor writings to bind their agreements. No Indian was ever known to tell an untruth."

This is the description the Greek historian and philosopher, Arrian, gives of the Indian character in ancient times.

India then fell on evil days. Prolonged spells of subjugation to foreign rule subverted the morale of the people and caused unbelievable national deterioration. Words, such as Arrian's, became the faint intimations of a remote, unreal past. But centuries later India exacted a tribute as magnificent as the one paid by Arrian and, in a way, even more significant.

The latter-day attester is not a friend, but an enemy - Qazi Nur Muhammad - who came to India with Ahmad Shah Durrani's seventh incursion into the country (1764-65) and was a witness to the Sikhs' battles with the invader. In his poetic account, in Persian, of the Durrani's invasion, he referred to the Sikhs in a rude and imprecatory language, but could not at the same time help proclaiming their many natural virtues. He said:

Do not call the "dogs" [His contumelious term for Sikhs] dogs, for they are lion, and are courageous like lions in the field of battle. How can a hero, who roars like a lion in the field of battle, be called a dog? If you wish to learn the art of war, come and face them in the field. They will demonstrate it to you in such a way that one and all will praise them for it...*Singh* is a title [a form of address] for them...If you do not know the Hindustani language, I shall tell you that the word *Singh* means a lion. Truly, they are like lions in battle and, in times of peace, they surpass Hatim in generosity.

Leaving aside their mode of fighting, hear ye another point in which they excel all other fighting people. In no case would they slay a coward, nor would they put an obstacle in the way of a fugitive. They do not plunder the wealth and ornaments of a woman, be she a well-to-do lady or a maid-servant. There is not adultery among these "dogs"...they do not make friends with adulterers and house-breakers.

For a people engaged in a life-and-death struggle strictly to observe such scruples was proof of their extraordinary moral discipline. It seems as if the gap of centuries had been made up. This resurrection of the national character was the result of the miracle wrought by Guru Gobind Singh.

The germ of this revolution lay in the gospel of human dignity preached by Guru Nanak. Guru Gobind Singh, Nanak X, brought to culmination the process of regeneration which had been started. He restored to the people, freshly affranchised by the teachings of his predecessors, their spiritual certitude and their qualities of resoluteness and sacrifice and revived their native energies. Judging from the cohesion he gave to the social fabric and from the transcendent nature of his undertaking towards raising the plane of man's thinking and action, Guru Gobind Singh ranks as the most constructive and charismatic genius in world history.

He truly perceived the causes of the people's downfall and the principles which could be the basis of reform and reclamation. One fundamental flaw was the lack of unity, of one common feeling of fellowship. The society was divided into sharply marked strata, mutually exclusive of one another. The country, as such, failed to reach to the frequent foreign invasions that took place. Whoever came conquered. Whatever resistance was offered was local or casual in character. No appeal to patriotism was possible, nor was any united action practicable.

When Guru Gobind Singh inherited the spiritual ministry of Guru Nanak, the Mughal rule in India was already a century and-a-half old. The founder, a homeless adventurer, had blundered into India without any substantial means. Yet he stayed on to establish an extensive and powerful empire. A foreign despotism reared on a rigid feudalistic structure was becoming increasingly oppressive. The Indian society had fallen back upon its built-in reserves for survival, but there was no positive response, nor any show of resistance or rebellion. Listlessness and an exclusive concern with personal salvation had become embedded in the national psyche, making any joint enterprise for political or social resuscitation impossible.

Guru Gobind Singh, building upon the heritage he had received from the preceding Gurus, brought about a remarkable change in the character of the people and lifted them out of their torpidity. By raising a strong voice of protest against political tyranny and religious intolerance and devising vigorous means to resist them, he aroused a firm spirit of patriotism. By preaching the common brotherhood of man and by taking practical steps to realize this ideal, he rejuvenated the social order ridding it of all kinds of inequalities. The Khalsa baptism he introduced became the elixir for a reinvigorated life – a life informed with social sensitivity and dedicated to the common cause. Whoever partook of it was fired with courage and zeal for sacrifice and considered himself equal to a whole army. He sloughed off his exclusivism and insularity, and established his kinship with a wider brotherhood. The Guru was the centre of his adoration and devotion. He gave him and the Khalsa commonwealth he had founded his whole-hearted allegiance, waiving his centuries-old complex of withdrawal and self-flagellation. The sword was the new profession he cultivated, and he must never be chary of using the weapon in defence of faith and justice. He must, of course, be equally careful not to use it for aggression. A new concept of life was thus born. Fearlessness, philanthropy and faith in God and the Guru and in a most exacting ethical code were its main ingredients.

The spirit created by Guru Gobind Singh was put to the severest trial in the years following his passing away in 1708. For almost a whole century, his followers suffered untold oppression and misery at the hands of the rulers, who were determined to scourge and extirpate the entire sect. They were outlawed and ordered to be killed at sight. Civic life was rendered impossible for them and they had to leave their homes, seeking shelter in the hills and jungles. Rewards were offered for their heads and their temples were either locked or demolished. Thousands of them were hanged, drawn and quartered. But they remained unvanquished and their spirit only toughened under the impact of every fresh calamity. They matched the situation with a rare power of endurance and won supreme moral exaltation by their heroic fight and suffering. They sanctified this period of their history with deeds of unparalleled sacrifice and bravery, and the Sikh character presented in this testing time its noblest aspect. In the midst of direst struggle, they never went back on their high-minded religious ideal nor forswore their spirit of magnanimity.

To die fighting for the principles sanctioned by Guru Gobind Singh and for the glory of the Khalsa was a consummation most cheerfully sought; to compromise with injustice was considered the extreme of degradation and pusillanimity. This brave new spirit generated a revolutionary impulse in the country and gave a new direction to the course of Indian history. When Shah Zaman, the grandson of Ahmad Shah Durrani, reached Peshawar on 30 January 1799, harassed and plundered by the Sikhs on his homeward journey after his Indian adventure, history had taken a decisive turn. No more invaders came into India from the north-west as they had been doing for centuries.

Once Nadir Shah, the Persian invader of India, questioned the Governor of Lahore who these Sikhs were. To which the latter made answer in this wise:

"They are a group of *faqirs*, who visit their Guru's tank twice a year and, bathing in it, disappear."

"Where do they live?" asked Nadir.

"Their homes are their horses' saddles," was the reply.

"Then take care," said Nadir, "for the day is not distant when these people will take possession of thy country."

Nadir was not far wrong in his warning. The Sikh came out of their jungle homes to establish gradually their sway in the country. When at last Ranjit Singh, a leader of great military prowess and political astuteness, occupied Lahore in 1799, they had laid the foundation of a powerful kingdom.

What is really significant about this historical curve is not so much the climactic point reached as the process of spiritual rebirth which lay behind it. This was the fulfilment and authentication of the Sikh prophecy and the measure of its power to transform the souls of men. Guru Gobind Singh taught the people to participate in the affairs of the world, making the truly religious values the basis of their behaviour and actions. Nothing less than complete adherence to them was acceptable. This led to a unique elevation of human conduct and to the unfolding of man's potentialities. A new inspiration, a new way of life grew out of this experimentation. Guru Gobind Singh's Khalsa was the manifestation of this moral resurgence.

This was Guru Gobind Singh's greatest contribution to human progress. He provided a truly moral and religious motive for men's actions and achieved a remarkable synthesis of the spiritual and the material, of the eternal and the temporal. He emancipated their minds from the bondage of dogma and superstition and released their energies for fearless and positive endeavour. He galvanized a dispirited and politically subdued people into bold and confident action, and turned them into a very potent force in history. Lovingly called by his followers the Lord of the Plume and the Lord of the White Hawk, he made the common man the inheritor of plumes and hawks - the symbols of sovereignty. In whatever condition they happened to be, a living faith in the Timeless Being was to be their guide and sustenance. Whether in adversity or prosperity, the highest standard of conduct and morality was to be maintained. This refashioning of the human spirit and character was the most significant achievement of Guru Gobind Singh's genius.

Apart from his historical role as the creator of a framework of high social and ethical values and of an order dedicated to the principles of religious belief and moral and heroic action Guru Gobind Singh's personal splendour and aura are a remarkable phenomenon. It is difficult to imagine a genius more comprehensive and versatile. In the words of the Muslim historian, Syed Muhammad Latif, Guru Gobind Singh "was a lawgiver in the pulpit, a champion in the field, a king on his *masnad* and a faqir in the society of the Khalsa."

He was a prophet with a full awareness of his divine purpose and an intense love of the people, a kingly patron of learning and a poet of deep spiritual insight, a natural leader of men and soldier of unmatched military prowess and courage, a social reformer and liberator and a saint with a wide human sympathy. He felt deeply the people, pain and suffering, and made the greatest sacrifices to secure alleviation. The words he had spoken as a child – innocently, but purposefully – proved so reassuring for his father, Guru Tegh Bahadur, a carrying out his resolve to lay down his life for the vindication of the principles of justice and freedom. He himself sacrificed his four sons, and so much besides, to fulfill the historical task to which he had committed himself and his followers. He created the instruments of a far-reaching social revolution and underwent in this process dramatic variations of fortune. Yet under all circumstances he retained his spiritual equanimity and set a superb example of stern moral action.

Whether he was at Anandpur riding his handsome blue charger, his regal plume setting of his wiry and commanding figure, with a knightly body of devoted and daring Sikhs following him, or in the jungle of Machhiwara, barefoot and forlorn, his heart was constantly in harmony with the Divine, neither losing its qualities of love and compassion in one situation, nor giving way to despair in the other.

Another important aspect of Guru Gobind Singh's genius was its poetic vitality. Just as he directed his practical prowess to the establishment of truth and justice, he used the medium of poetry to deliver the divine revelation. Not all of his verse has come down to us; a considerable part of it was lost in the turbulent days of his later career. Mercifully, there is still enough of it to reveal the uncanny power and range of his poetic utterance and its spiritual efficacy. His poetry is unexcelled for its immediacy, freshness and vigour. In proclaiming the supreme holiness and majesty of God it remains unsurpassed in any language. Another point of note lies on its descriptions of the scenes of battle. The sounds and fury of raging action – its tempo and heat as well as the clashing of steel emitting metallic clangour and sparks – are recaptured in vivid and evocative verbal and metrical patterns which have an overpowering physical impact. Guru Gobind Singh thus created meaningful imagery both of worship and chivalry. For its intellectual sweep, granite-like quality and rhythm, his poetry is so different from the literary creation of the period marked by effervescent and inconsequential sentimentalism.

Prophet, poet, soldier, philosopher, prince and recluse, Guru Gobind Singh is lovingly remembered for his deep humanity and compassion. He played within the brief span of forty-two years a wide diversity of roles with extraordinary resource and purposefulness. Over the years, he has become a most eloquent symbol of all that is virile and positive in our religious tradition. Visions of glory are conjured up as that vital, many splendoured image, beplumed and enrobed, saintly symbols and badges claiming precedence with soldierly regalia, emerges before our eyes from the folds of history. It is the centre of the Sikhs' memory of their origin and tradition and a perennial source of inspiration for them. It still stimulates among them a peculiar kind of spiritual upsurge and they have always felt the presence of the Master – Soul among them. In the crucial moments of their more recent history, the Lord of the White Hawk was as tangibly their hero and guiding-star as he had been during the time of his earthly existence.

Guru Gobind Singh's work is best understood as the fulfilment of Guru Nanak's mission. Explaining the purpose of his life in the *Bachitra Natak*, Guru Gobind Singh said:

For this purpose was I born,
Understand all ye pious people,
To uphold righteousness, to protect those worthy and virtuous.
To overcome and destroy the evil-doers.

Guru Gobind Singh had set himself against oppression and intolerance. He did not fight for any territory or worldly power, or against any religion or sect. Among his admires and followers were Hindus as well as Muslims. Many staunch followers of Islam had aligned themselves with him against the imperial armies. Pir Buddhu Shah sacrificed two of his sons and a number of his disciples in the battle of Bhangani fighting on his side. The Muslim ruler of Malerkotla, Nawab Sher Muhammad Khan, raised a strong protest against the execution of his two minor sons at Sirhind. Thus people of different faiths were attracted to the Guru whose teaching was that all men were equal and that, though outer forms differed, the fundamental truth was the same everywhere.

The Sikh organization took on the semblance of a state during Guru Gobind Singh's days. But amidst all its splendour, he maintained almost puritanical standards of simplicity in his personal life. Guru Nanak had started his work on a softer note, but no one could mistake its sternness and implacability towards injustice, cruelty and hypocrisy. What happened in the time of Guru Gobind Singh was a natural consequence of the peculiar situation he was confronted with. His life's work has sometimes been misinterpreted and the martial spirit inculcated by him regarded as a reversal of teaching of the founder of the faith. This is a wholly an erroneous view. Guru Gobind Singh took up arms only to defend the religious values established by the Gurus preceding him, the values which his father and grandfather had upheld at the cost of their lives. None of the battles he fought was of his seeking, nor did he attempt to annex any territory in consequence of his military successes. His struggle against injustice and tyranny was in keeping with the spirit of the teachings of Guru Nanak, who had himself censured clearly and unmistakably the oppression practised by the Mughal invaders. The inner principle of Sikhism, as determined by the founder and substantiated by the eight succeeding Gurus, was brought to its highest fulfilment by the last, Guru Gobind Singh.

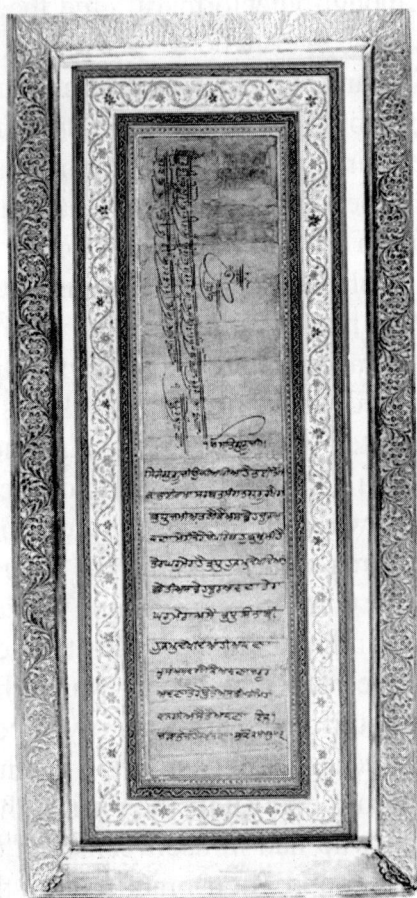

Hukamnama of Guru Gobind Singh
bestowed on the House of Phulkian

Chronology

1666, December 26	Birth of Guru Gobind Singh
1675, July 12	Arrest of Guru Tegh Bahadur at Malikpur Rangharan
1675, November 11	Martyrdom of Guru Tegh Bahadur in Chandni Chowk, Delhi
1684	*Var Sri Bhagauti ji ki* (*Chandi di Var*) completed
1685, April 14	Guru Gobind Singh reached Nahan
1685, April 29	Foundation of Paonta laid
1687, January 26	Sahibzada Ajit Singh born
1687, September 4	Baba Ram Rai passed away
1688, September 18	Battle of Bhangani
1691, March 14	Birth of Sahibzada Jujhar Singh
1691, March 20	Battle of Nadaun
1696, February 20	Battle against Hussain Khan
1696, July 13	Prince Muazzam deputed to settle Punjab affairs
1696, August	*Hukumnama*, addressed to Bhais Tilok Singh and Ram Singh
1696, November 17	Birth of Sahibzada Zorawar Singh
1698	Completion of *Bachitra Natak*
1699, February 25	Birth of Sahibzada Fateh Singh
1699, March 30	(Baisakhi) – Creation of Khalsa
1700, June 26	First Battle of Anandpur
1700, October 8	Battle of Nirmoh

1701	Mata Jitoji passed away
1703, December 2	Second Battle of Anandpur
1704, Winter	Third Battle of Anandpur
1705, December 5-6 (night)	Anandpur evacuated
1705, December 7	Battle of Chamkaur
1705, December 9	Guru Gobind Singh's younger sons refuse to obey Nawab Wazir Khan's orders
1705, December 12	Guru Gobind Singh's younger son martyred
1705, December 29	Battle of Muktsar
1706, January 20	Guru Gobind Singh arrived at Talwandi Sabo
1706, October 30	Guru Gobind Singh left Damdama (Talwandi Sabo)
1707, February 20	Emperor Aurangzeb died
1707, June 8	Battle of Jajau
1707, July 23	Meeting with Bahadur Shah
1707, October 2	Letter to the *sangat* of Dhaul
1708, August	Guru Gobind Singh arrived at Nander
1708, September 3	Madho Das (Banda Singh) baptized
1708, October 6	*Granth Sahib* declared Guru Eternal
1708, October 7	Guru Gobind Singh left for heavenly abode

Index